The Sunday

A to Z Gu

FAMILY FINANCE

The Sunday Telegraph
A to Z Guide to
FAMILY FINANCE

Damian Reece

HEADLINE

Copyright © 1996 The Telegraph plc and Damian Reece

Line illustrations by Martin Honeysett

First published in 1996
by HEADLINE BOOK PUBLISHING

10 9 8 7 6 5 4 3 2 1

ISBN 0 7472 7839 3

Typeset by
Letterpart Ltd, Reigate, Surrey

Printed and bound in Great Britain by
Mackays of Chatham PLC, Chatham, Kent

HEADLINE BOOK PUBLISHING
A division of Hodder Headline PLC
338 Euston Road
London NW1 3BH

Contents

To Page

Author's Foreword

Money is perhaps the biggest consumer issue of them all. The mass media pays much attention to concerns such as health and education – quite rightly – but the pound in your pocket and what happens to it have the most fundamental and long-lasting effect on your future.

This book explains the world of money as it affects you, the consumer. Being an A to Z guide it aims to cater for the novice, yet anyone who has crossed paths with the financial services industry but is not really conversant with how this £500bn mega-business works will find it useful. Its plain-English style will help give everyone a firm grip on the world of money.

The book covers all aspects of the financial world from the simplest insurance contract to the national debt, from European monetary union to investments you can profit from, as well as the workings of the City of London. Significant terms are highlighted in **bold**.

Parts of this guide appeared in the *Sunday Telegraph* in weekly instalments in 1995 and my thanks must go to Neil Simpson, Liz Dolan, Ron Emler and Gordon Hopkins of the *Sunday Telegraph* finance team for their help in the preparation of that series. The series was produced in association with TSB Bank PLC, and the *Sunday Telegraph* is very grateful for their contribution. As with the series, this book has been written with no editorial influence from TSB.

A is for:

ACCIDENT INSURANCE

A gory subject to start with but one that parents or people with dependants should think about. This type of insurance normally pays an agreed lump sum whenever the policyholder suffers as a result of an accident. There are ghoulish scales of payment which reflect the seriousness of the injuries – so losing a finger could pay £10,000, losing an eye £50,000 and total disablement £100,000.

But why take out such insurance? Most people have **life assurance** which provides cash on a policyholder's death to ease the burden on those left behind. Fewer people, however, consider the likelihood of suffering a serious accident that could keep them from work for long periods, and it is at times like this that extra cash comes in useful to pay the household bills or provide specialist equipment needed by an injured person.

Premiums can be quite modest and average about £50 a year, while more limited **accidental death policies** are often given away free by banks or building societies. Also, people who take up the offer of free insurance can often increase their cover at a discount.

Parents or grandparents can buy policies to cover children, and some schools give details of policies covering accidents on

Sports insurers can cover high-risk activites including white-water rafting, off-piste skiing and bungee jumping

playing fields and on trips. Specialist sports insurance can provide cover for high-risk activities which are excluded from standard life or health insurance policies – these can include everything from white-water rafting to off-piste skiing and bungee jumping.

Reputable insurance brokers can find policies or people can call insurance companies direct. The British Insurance and Investment Brokers' Association will give the name and address of a local broker – its hot line is listed in the useful numbers section.

ACTUARY

Often considered the most boring people in the world doing the world's most boring job – unless you are an actuary of course – actuaries are the number crunchers par excellence of the insurance world. Actuarial calculations are long, complex and very dull but have tremendous impact on our lives. Actuaries assess risk and put a price on insuring against an event happening. In a way they are laying odds, like a bookmaker, against something occurring. Death, for instance, is their most popular subject and assessing the risk or likelihood of someone's death happening has a great fascination for actuaries. They are experts on life expectancy. An actuary calculates someone's life expectancy bearing in mind such things as medical evidence, occupation, sex, and age. A price or premium is then set depending on how likely that person's death is. So the shorter your expected life span, the more expensive things such as life assurance become. Although the image is of grey men in even greyer suits, the actuarial profession can lead to very well-paid, high-flying careers at the top of big insurance companies – if you like that sort of thing.

ADVICE

If I could grant one wish to all the people who have asked me for help with their money affairs it would be a reliable source of impartial and trustworthy financial advice – a financial genie no less. Is this just wishful thinking on my part or is it really possible to find such a fairy-tale financial adviser? Someone who will be around for years to come, have an in-depth understanding of your affairs and your needs and be as honest as the day is long?

As a child I was always told never to trust men who wore bow ties or camelhair coats. Such a rule would have come in handy had I been one of those unlucky investors who came face to face with either Roger Levitt or Peter Clowes – two of the country's most infamous financial advisers who broke the rules and who both sported such garb on a regular basis. First impressions should not be underestimated. Gut instinct is all important.

But these days, finding a financial genie is supposed to be a little more scientific than simply casting a keen eye over their dress and office surroundings, although these are useful pointers to the efficiency and professionalism of an adviser. Most people who decide that the odd piece of avuncular advice or paternal share tip is not enough look for financial help from the high street, through either a bank or a building society. Some will know an accountant or solicitor who either claims to specialise in personal financial affairs or knows an adviser who does. Others will be approached by an insurance or investment company, often after responding to an advertisement.

Already the number of potential sources of advice – and thus of rogues – is mind boggling. Luckily Parliament thinks so too and introduced the **Financial Services Act** to control the affairs of advisers, which took effect in 1988. This means that all financial advisers have to be regulated and must produce proper identification to prove their bona fides. There are two basic types of financial adviser, **tied** and **independent**. Their business cards must make it clear what their status is, and this can make a big difference to the advice customers are given.

As the name suggests, *tied advisers* (otherwise known as tied agents or direct salesmen) are linked to one insurance or investment company and can only sell that company's products. They will normally be described as 'an appointed agent of' a certain insurer on their business cards. They have to decide which of the company's products is best for their client but cannot recommend products from rivals, even if their own policies are bad value for money. If none of their company's products are suitable for a person's circumstances they are supposed to say so and end the interview. Conversely, *independent financial advisers* (IFAs) are not linked to any single company and have to prove that they have considered all the products in the marketplace before recommending one to a client. Their business cards will normally show that they are members of the **Personal Investment Authority**, which is their Government-appointed regulatory body, and many will carry a blue logo saying that their companies are members of the lobby group IFA Promotions. Stockbrokers, solicitors and accountants can also offer financial advice and often have specialist independent advisers on their staffs.

The argument about which type of financial advice is better – independent or tied – has been raging for many years. On the surface, IFAs who can give impartial advice ought to be the better bet. But they have their drawbacks. Many of them are small, one-man-band operators with little in the way of financial resources. They regularly go out of business at one whiff of a recession or regulatory crackdown, leaving clients to find a new adviser. Moreover, like everyone, IFAs need to make a crust, and this they do out of the commission they earn when selling insurance or investment products. Unfortunately, this method of earning inevitably means that some IFAs will sell people unnecessary products just to earn commission.

There is also the question of **churning**. This is one threat the budding financial consumer can watch out for. Churning is the nasty habit practised by some IFAs of switching clients in and out of policies needlessly just to pocket the commission this generates. If you are being switched from one policy or investment to another every few months you are probably the victim of churning.

Tied advisers, on the other hand, tend to work for the big insurers and banks. While they are limited to recommending just their employer's products, they can still provide a full and objective assessment of your financial needs. Certainly the arguments about churning and generating sales just for the commission apply to the tied adviser as much as to the IFA, but tied advisers are backed by the multimillion, sometimes multibillion pound businesses of their employers who are increasingly strict about how their tied advisers operate.

If a tied salesman works for a company with competitive

products that perform well, consumers are probably losing little to the clients of many IFAs. Another advantage of the tied sector is that the insurers and investment companies involved will probably be around for the rest of your life, supplying ongoing advice, which is something many IFAs simply will not be able to do. And of course, for many consumers, dealing with the tied advisers of one or two big insurers is all they want and need. It is a question of taste.

However, as commercial pressures have forced many small IFAs out of business, the surviving ones are getting bigger. There is now a breed of super-IFAs, often the subsidiary of one of the big insurers or banks, which are very well resourced and controlled. They can give a very impressive hi-tech service which will be available for as long as you need it.

Big IFAs will also be willing to work on a fee basis rather than sales commission, which is rebated back to the fee-paying consumer. Fees, which are charged per hour and vary depending on the complexity of advice being given, range from £30 to £150 per hour. The advantage of fees is that advisers are under no pressure to make sales and thus earn commission. After assessing your needs they can advise you not to take any action at all, without any financial loss to them personally.

Few advisers want cheques for insurance policies or investment plans made out to themselves and customers should be wary of doing so. In most cases it is safer and more efficient for a cheque to be made out to the recommended insurer or investment company and the adviser will pass it on.

So what questions should you ask to help pick the best adviser and avoid the cowboys? Well, you can start with the following list:

1. Are you an independent financial adviser or are you tied to a single insurance company?
2. Is the adviser regulated, and, if so, by whom and can they prove it? The main regulators are the Personal Investment Authority (PIA) and its parent the **Securities and Investments Board**. You will find their details at the back of this

book. The PIA can tell you if someone claiming to be an adviser is registered. If your choice is not on the list, you should be wary of using that adviser.
3. How long has the adviser been in business and how big is the company he or she works for? Small is not necessarily bad, but consumers need to think about how long their chosen adviser is going to be around for.
4. What are the adviser's strengths and weaknesses?
5. Will they make money out of commission or will you pay a fee for advice?

The telephone number for a list of fee-charging IFAs is listed at the back of the book.

Once you have picked your adviser, if things then turn sour – perhaps because of their poor administration or bad advice – there are various compensation and complaints schemes consumers can go through to obtain redress. These procedures are covered more fully later in the book under R for Regulators. The big financial advice scandals have generally involved IFAs – Knight Williams, Noble Lowndes (now part of the Sedgwick insurance group which was fined £740,000 in 1993 for various rule breaches including bad advice), the Levitt Group, Barlow Clowes, and so on. While independent advice is laudable, caution must be exercised when taking that advice.

ALTERNATIVE INVESTMENTS

Shares and houses are the most popular investments with the British, but our innate eccentricity means that we find lots of other weird and wonderful things to throw our money at in the – normally vain – hope of making a fortune. Some people invest in anything from paintings and wine to racehorses, forests, stamps, gold coins and theatre productions. Ostrich farming is a recent and bizarre addition to the list. Returns on such investments can be high, but there are no guarantees – sadly, life's pleasures rarely make good investments. Experts say people considering alternative investments have to know their markets and be prepared to lose their shirts.

Many alternative investment schemes are promoted as serious investments with full and complex prospectuses. But there are rarely any safety nets as the plans are not covered by the protective cloak of the Financial Services Act. Therefore, before taking the plunge with an investment in bloodstock, African art, or whatever, it is worth asking yourself a few general questions. For example:

- Are the assets you are buying limited in supply?
- Are the assets easy to manage?
- Is ownership expensive because of special insurance requirements or storage and maintenance?
- Can you sell your investment easily to realise any gains?
- Is there a reputable and objective way of valuing the assets?
- Are there any tax benefits to the investment?

The **Society of London Theatre** can advise prospective theatre investors and the **Racehorse Owners Association** can help people wanting to make money from owning all or part of a horse. Interest in the art market has been picking up, with auction houses Christie's and Sotheby's reporting strong demand since the art market crash of 1990–91. The improvement is based on an increase in interest for Impressionist and twentieth-century art.

Ostriches, however, are a rather different prospect. Farms have been set up recently to exploit what has been called the 'cash crop of the 1990s'. Some farms are advertising returns of more than 50 per cent plus annual income, with easy payment plans to buy 'breeder chicks'.

Buying antiques as an investment is risky and can affect other areas of financial planning. Standard house contents insurance policies may have small print excluding cover for unusual items. But there may be compensations. Specialist policies exist for people with antiques or high-value contents and the premiums can work out cheaper than those on standard policies. For insurers say that people with high-value house contents tend to take more care with security, so are less likely to be burgled. Their insurance premiums thus reflect the reduced risk of claims.

Alternative investments should only be tried once safer, more orthodox investment and savings routes have been exhausted. Nevertheless, this is unlikely to deter the committed philatelist or numismatist from piling in to Penny Blacks or Roman coins. Enjoyment should be a big feature of any alternative investment.

ANNUITIES

The good news about annuities is that they give retired people an income for the rest of their lives. The bad news is that once bought, annuities cannot be changed or refunded – so people should check they are getting a good deal when they buy.

People pay a lump sum to an insurer and are promised a set monthly, quarterly or annual income for the rest of their lives. In most cases the money paid out will not be returned even if the buyer dies almost immediately after handing it over. The amount of income paid depends ultimately on the level of **interest rates** when the annuity is bought, so the best rates are offered when interest rates are high. Standard annuities invest in **gilt-edged securities** issued by the government that pay a fixed and secure income. Returns available on gilts are dictated mainly by interest rates.

As the money is paid for life, insurers offer the best rates to older people. Women receive a lower income than men of the same age as they are likely to live several years longer. People in poor health are often offered better annuity rates as the insurer assumes they will not survive to claim many payments. People wanting such **impaired life annuities** have to give medical evidence to their chosen annuity provider.

In the past, the rules meant people had to buy an annuity

with their pension fund as soon as they retired and took a tax-free lump sum. This is great for people who retire when annuity rates are high, but works against those who retire when they are low. The Inland Revenue has relaxed the rules, however, and will now allow people with a **personal pension** to postpone buying an annuity until they think rates are high enough. People can draw an income from their pension fund in the meantime. The change is welcome and is likely to be extended to **company pension** schemes, but people may lose out by delaying and should get proper advice before doing so.

There are several different types of annuities, and many options and extras can be attached to them.

The most common type of annuity is the **compulsory purchase annuity** or **pension annuity**. This is bought on retirement with a pension fund built up in a company or personal pension plan. When the company or personal pension firm sends out a pension statement on retirement it says how much income it would give on its own annuity scheme. But people are free to shop around among other insurers to get better rates. The technical term for shopping around is to exercise an **open market option**. It almost always pays to do so. The difference between the best and worst annuity payers can be as much as 30 per cent – and remember that this money is paid every year for the rest of the person's life. Thus someone who forgets to shop around, takes an annuity of £10,000 a year and then survives for 20 years could end up £60,000 worse off than someone who retired on the same day and lived as long but who found a better paying annuity company on retirement.

Many people want more than their compulsory purchase annuity and use other money to buy a second annuity. These are called **purchased life annuities** and have tax benefits as some of the income is treated as a return of capital. People do not have to spend all their pension funds on an annuity: 25–30 per cent of those funds can be taken as a tax-free lump sum. But some people choose to spend this lump sum on a purchased life annuity to boost their income. This type of annuity provides income taxed at a lower rate than income from a pension annuity because some of the payments are treated as a tax-free return of capital. A good financial adviser can explain the benefits. However, one set of options concerns the different ways of paying income – monthly payments produce about 7 per cent less than annual income providers. Payments can also be in advance or in arrears and it costs more to get the money early. Annuities paying money monthly in advance produce about 1 per cent less than those paying monthly in arrears, while annuities paying annually in advance pay about 15 per cent less than those paying annually in arrears.

Annuities can be bought with a **guaranteed period,** normally of between five and ten years. These annuities promise that an income will be paid until the end of the guaranteed period even if the buyer dies beforehand. The money can be paid as a lump sum or in regular payments and goes into the annuity-holder's estate. The cost of a guaranteed period is reduced income. **Spouses, dependants or joint-life** annuities also help to protect income and ensure that it does not all die with the annuity-holder.

Most annuities pay a fixed amount of income for the buyer's lifetime. But it is possible to pay more and have payments index-linked. **Escalating annuities** increase the income by a set amount each year but are expensive. A 60-year-old man wanting an annuity with a 5 per cent escalation would be paid 42 per cent less in the first year than he would on a level plan. The best advice for anyone approaching retirement age is to shop around for the best annuity rate and the most suitable package. Specialist annuity brokers can help.

$\mathcal{B}$ is for:

BANKS

Love them or hate them, Britain's high-street banks provide the bulk of most people's personal finance needs: current accounts, savings accounts, mortgages or personal loans. The facts behind the banking system are impressive. For example:

- Last year 95 per cent of UK adults had a bank or **building society** current account, compared with just 50 per cent in 1982.
- Each day £105bn is 'cleared' through the UK's banks.
- This includes 8m cheques and 7m automated transactions through 14,500 cash machines.

Businesses this size produce very big profits as well as very big mail bags full of complaints. As banks' profits have soared since the slump in the early 1990s the number of complaints against them has risen. In 1994 the combined profits of the 'big four' high-street banks – Barclays, Lloyds, Midland and NatWest – hit nearly £5bn while telephone complaints about banks reached nearly 20,000, according to the **Banking Ombudsman** (the place to go with a complaint that a bank has not settled to your satisfaction).

The once cosy relationship between a customer and their bank manager is on the wane. Bank managers are these days often no more than glorified insurance salesmen. Banks see themselves as one-stop financial supermarkets offering everything from current accounts to investments to tax planning. They have built up big insurance subsidiaries, which branch managers are expected to promote. The term **bancassurance** has sprung up to describe the modern-day bank and many people do not like the monolithic nature of these organisations. Many of the traditional functions of the local bank branch such as lending decisions have been centralised at regional level, reducing a bank's links with people and small businesses.

In the face of such criticism banks are trying to change. Branches have become more pleasant places to do business and services such as telephone banking have been introduced to satisfy the demands of customers. But technology is changing so fast that bank branches and even telephone banking will be superseded by the concept of **virtual banking**. This is banking without the branch or the telephone but transacted via personal computer or interactive cable television. Personal contact will still be available but this will be done via screen-based technology, so that you can talk to your bank manager and see him at the same time without having to leave your home.

The banks at the heart of the money flow are called **clearing banks**, which handle vast sums and as a result have to combat fraud on a vast scale. Some idea of the scope for this fraud can be had from the following statistics:

- Each day people make 3m cash withdrawals over the counters of the country's 11,000 bank branches.
- The branches employ 280,000 people.
- Banks have issued 26m credit, debit and cash point cards.
- They were hit by card fraud worth £96m in 1994, a drop on the 1993 figure of £129m.

The Bank of England, nicknamed the Old Lady of Threadneedle Street, oversees the banks and is responsible for authorising and monitoring them. Most people are well aware of the big high-street banks but few realise that there are in fact 525 institutions authorised under the 1987 Banking Act. They include the City of London investment banks, which deal with the banking needs of companies and governments as well as local authorities and other large institutions. Investment banks raise share and loan capital for their customers and advise on matters such as takeovers and mergers. They also have big fund management operations managing money for individuals, charities and pension funds.

As well as the high-street chains, the world of banks includes the very posh and the very obscure. People who feel like paying for a bit of cosseting and impressively embossed note paper can go to the **private banks** such as Coutts, or C. Hoare & Co. Even Harrods has its own bank. Private banks can serve a useful purpose for wealthy individuals whose affairs are unusually complex and who need individual and time-consuming attention. UK banks also include such strange-sounding organisations as the Thai Farmers Bank and the Assemblies of God Property Trust.

The Bank of England (simply known as the Bank by most people) authorises institutions as deposit takers. It also monitors bank lending to try and ensure depositors' funds are not at risk. The Bank does not guarantee a bank's obligations should it get into difficulties, although a big enough crash might result in a government bail-out. Some banks such as the high-street clearers are said to be 'too big to fail'.

In normal circumstances the customers of a collapsed bank must rely on a rescue by another financial institution as happened with the ruined investment bank Baring Brothers, victim of rogue Singapore employee Nick Leeson. Barings was bought out by the Dutch Bank ING. The alternative is the **Deposit Protection Scheme**, which pays out a portion of a customer's deposits in a collapsed bank. Recent examples of bail-outs include the **Bank of Credit and Commerce International (BCCI)** and **Wimbledon & South West Finance**. The maximum payout under the scheme is 90 per cent of deposits held by any one individual, up to £20,000.

This means the maximum possible payout is £18,000, so only partial cover is provided, unless wealthy people split their deposits up between different banks placing £20,000 with each.

BASE RATE

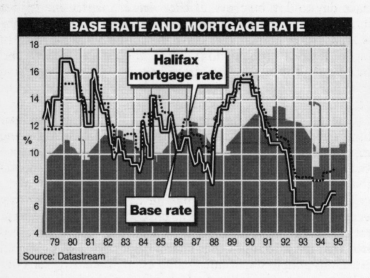

BASE RATE AND MORTGAGE RATE

Halifax mortgage rate

Base rate

Source: Datastream

This sets the general level of interest rates in the UK and is perhaps the most crucial single weapon in the government's economic armoury. It is controlled by the Chancellor of the Exchequer and implemented by the Bank of England. Every month the Chancellor meets with the Bank Governor to discuss economic policy and the views expressed on interest rates normally prove the most forthright.

The base rate is central to the Chancellor's attempts to regulate the economy in order to keep it running smoothly – not too fast and not too slow. A base-rate rise will be used to cool the economy when prices and growth are rising too fast. A base-rate fall is designed to stimulate economic activity. The alternative to using base rates to control the economy is the politically more sensitive policy of taxation, that is, lower taxes for higher growth and vice versa.

The official name for the base rate is the **Minimum Lending Rate**. This is the rate at which the Bank of England will lend money to the big high-street and investment banks. These banks are typically in need of extra cash or liquidity to run their day-to-day business. If they are forced to pay higher interest on money borrowed from the Bank of England, they will pass these higher costs on to the consumer in the form of higher interest rates for loans and overdrafts to people and businesses. This makes the cost of borrowing dearer, reducing spending and investments and thus slowing down economic activity.

One of the most important ways in which chancellors have tried to control the economy is through the housing market. Because so many Britons have borrowed money to buy their own home their spending habits are highly sensitive to changes in interest rates. Interest payments on mortgages are often a very large part of a household's monthly expenditure. Any increase in the cost of mortgages will have an immediate impact on people's spending habits. It is also true that the price of houses has an important psychological effect on people's spending patterns. It is the biggest contributor to the so-called **feelgood factor** that has been so noticeably missing in recent years. If the price of your house is rising you are bound to feel better off and therefore more confident to go out and spend.

You may have noticed how quick banks and building societies are to pass on base rate rises in the form of higher borrowing costs but are somewhat slower to pass on to savers the other effect of a base rate rise which is higher investment rates. Over the past 15 years another trend has come to light that shows mortgage rates peaking at higher levels relative to base rates. When the **Thatcher government** hoisted base rates to 17 per cent in 1980, lenders such as the Halifax put up lending rates to 15 per cent, comfortably below base rates.

When base rates next peaked in 1984 they rose to 14 per cent and Halifax's mortgage rate also hit 14 per cent. In the most recent cycle, base rates peaked at 15 per cent in 1990 but Halifax's rate rose to 15.4 per cent. This trend can be traced on the graph on page 16. It is also true that at the bottom of the economic cycle when interest rates are at their lowest the base rate falls below the mortgage rate. There is typically a two percentage point difference.

BED AND BREAKFASTING

Bed and breakfasting is the sale and repurchase of shares to reduce capital gains tax

When stockbrokers talk about bed and breakfasting they are not discussing a weekend away in the countryside; a financial B&B is something much less racy. Bed and breakfasting is the sale and repurchase of shares to make best use of a person's annual exemption from capital gains tax, which currently allows you to make £6,300 of profits each year before the tax kicks in. Typically a person will sell enough shares to yield a £6,300 profit – on which no tax is payable – and then repurchase them. The repurchase establishes a higher cost value for the shares and this will help reduce future tax liabilities.

This financial manoeuvre is of interest only to people with investment portfolios big enough to generate annual profits or capital gains of £6,300 or more a year. When it comes to executing a B&B it is worth shopping around among a few stockbrokers as charges will vary, with some brokers offering cheap B&B deals at the end of a tax year when a B&B makes most sense.

BONDS

Bonds are important investments for people trying to generate income from their capital – for example, people in retirement. Bonds pay investors a fixed rate of interest, called a **coupon**, once or twice per year. Most bonds have fixed lives and at the end of a bond's life it matures and an investor's original capital is repaid, or at least that is the theory.

Some companies that issue bonds go bust leaving the bondholders with no capital and no income. The most recent group of bondholders to be left with nothing are those who invested in bonds issued by Baring Brothers. Although the rescue by Dutch Bank ING secured people's deposits it did not include the repayment or servicing of the bank's bonds. Other prominent corporate collapses which have left bondholders reeling include fruit and packaging company Polly Peck and financial services group British & Commonwealth.

As well as companies, bonds are issued by governments and local authorities. Bonds are a way of borrowing which avoids the need of turning to a bank for finance. In the UK, government bonds are called **gilt-edged securities**, dealt with in more detail later in the book.

The attraction of bonds is their regular and known interest payments, although there are risks. But if a bond issuer collapses, then the bondholders will almost always rank above the ordinary shareholders when it comes to gaining access to any remaining funds. Bonds issued by sound governments are considered more secure than those issued by companies, however big or successful. Indeed securities such as gilt-edged securities or the United States equivalent known as **T Bonds** are the closest you will come to a guaranteed investment. The different levels of risk associated with various bond issuers is reflected in the interest that investors demand.

Of UK bonds, gilts pay the lowest interest because they are perceived to be the least risky. Some companies have to pay a lot more interest to attract investors. Both gilts and bonds issued by public companies are listed on the stock market and can be bought and sold through a stockbroker. Gilts can also be bought from National Savings through the Post Office. They can be bought when first issued or later when dealing starts on the stock market. The price of bonds is influenced mainly by interest rates. If interest rates rise, deposit accounts become more attractive and bond prices fall and vice versa.

Investors who buy bonds when prices have fallen get more income for their money because a bond's fixed interest payments represent a larger percentage of the price paid. This percentage figure is known as a **bond's yield**. As bond prices rise, so their yields fall and investors have the chance to make capital gains. A rise in inflation will tend to cause bond prices to fall because fixed interest and capital payments become less attractive as their value is eroded.

BUILDING SOCIETIES

These august institutions are not as old as banks, which can trace their roots back to the 1600s, but they do date back to 1775. In the past ten years they have grown from being simple savings and mortgage providers into complex one-stop financial centres offering everything from personal banking and credit cards to insurance and stock-market-based investments.

They have become a central part of the rise of bancassurance on the high street. In fact banks have found building societies increasingly stiff competition since 1986 when the **Building Societies Act** gave them wider powers. Societies have since formed their own insurance companies, expanded into estate agency and have become fund managers and stockbrokers. In the process there have been a wave of mergers and takeovers.

In the past decade the number of societies has halved from 167 to 81. The most recent reductions in the statistics have resulted from the **Cheltenham & Gloucester** being taken over by **Lloyds Bank** and the largest society, the **Halifax**, merging with the **Leeds Permanent**. The merged group will then float on the stock market and become a bank similar to the former building society **Abbey National** which has bid for the **National & Provincial** building society. Now the **Woolwich** and **Alliance & Leicester** building societies have announced plans to become banks. This process of building societies disappearing from the movement is called **demutualisation**. Societies cease to be mutual organisations owned by their members (these are certain classes of savers and borrowers) and become instead publicly owned companies with shares quoted on the Stock Exchange like many banks.

In the merger mania gripping building societies at present some people have deposited money with various large and middle-sized societies. They hope to strike it lucky and share in bonus payments or free share issues handed out during demutualisation and have been dubbed '**carpet baggers**'. The recent mergers reflect the pressures building societies have felt from the weakness in the housing market and the rise in bad debts. They are also popular takeover targets because of their large financial reserves built up over many years, which as mutuals they find hard to exploit. Stock-market-quoted banks, on the other hand, can put these often huge sums to work in a variety of ways, assuming they can get their hands on them. This is one reason why banks have been willing to pay handsomely for the societies in the form of bonuses.

Several societies have been forced to merge with stronger and larger competitors. In 1991, for instance, the Leamington Spa merged with the Bradford & Bingley. This practice by which stronger societies rescue smaller ones is overseen by the **Building Societies Commission,** the sector's regulator. It means that stricken societies are not allowed to collapse but are propped up by the rest of the industry. As a result no building society customer has lost money through a collapse, unlike some bank customers. The building societies also have an extra layer of protection in the form of the **Investor Protection Scheme.** It pays out the same amount as the **Deposit Protection Scheme** for banks.

BULLS AND BEARS

These are creatures of the stock market rather than the forest. The terms describe two different types of investors. Bulls are optimists about market prices. They believe share prices will rise for the foreseeable future in what is known as a bull market. The term is most used about share markets but is also applied to bonds, currencies, commodities, interest rates and property. Someone who reckons the copper price will rise is bullish about copper.

On the other hand, bears are market pessimists who believe prices are going to fall. If they are correct, shares are said to be in a bear market. The most famous bear markets in this century came after the 1929 Wall Street crash in the United States as well as the prolonged downturn in prices during the early 1970s. The most celebrated bull market of recent years came in the mid-1980s. It ended with the crash on Black Monday – 19 October 1987.

C is for:

CAPITAL GAINS TAX

This is paid on profits from the sale of most physical and financial assets. Everyone can make £6,300 of capital gains each year tax-free, but after this the tax is charged at a person's income tax rate.

The Inland Revenue allows people to reduce their capital gains tax bill each year by subtracting losses from profits and it applies the tax to the net gain. It also allows inflation to be taken into account. Gains can be indexed when it comes to calculating a CGT bill and this means tax is paid only on real gains in value excluding inflation. Since November 1993 it is no longer possible to increase a loss by indexation and then subtract the indexed losses from any gains.

People can use an accountant's indexation table to calculate how inflation has reduced their liabilities. CGT tends to be paid on shares or other securities such as unit or investment trusts. The easiest way to avoid paying CGT is to use tax shelters such as **Personal Equity Plans** (Peps) and **Tax Exempt Special Savings Accounts** (Tessas).

The tax is also payable on the disposal of property such as holiday homes and assets such as works of art, vintage cars and gold. But not all gains will be hit by CGT. The Revenue carries a list of CGT exemptions, such as people's main domestic residence, private cars, National Lottery and football pools winnings, and horse race betting profits.

Losses for CGT purposes can be claimed when the Revenue deems a company's shares to be of negligible value. This allows investors to claim a loss without having to sell the shares and occurs when the company goes bust.

CAR INSURANCE

Many insurers refuse to cover those aged 25 or under, or people with high-performance cars or poor driving records

The bad news is that it is illegal to have a car on the road without insurance. The good news is that premiums are falling. Rising levels of theft and fraud were driving up premiums but the tide has turned. One reason is that insurers are forcing drivers to buy security systems to reduce theft and have compiled a register of frequent claimants to reduce fraud.

A further reason is stiff competition. Most drivers used to buy car insurance through brokers who would trawl the market for good deals or would buy from a salesman or agent employed by an insurance company. Inertia and stable premiums meant that people rarely moved. But in the past ten years **direct insurers** have sprung up, offering cut-price cover over the telephone. Direct insurers say they offer better rates by cutting out the middlemen, brokers, and costly sales networks. They use computer systems to sign up customers and handle claims. Direct insurance has turned the market round and several traditional insurers now compete through their own direct subsidiaries.

Brokers are also fighting back, using computers to shop around for deals and compete with direct firms by responding to enquiries within minutes. However, telephone insurers typically take care of paperwork, sending customers policy documents to sign when they have agreed the details over the telephone.

Traditional insurers, direct insurers and brokers all offer two types of cover: **third party fire and theft,** or **comprehensive**. Third party fire and theft pays for damage that drivers do to other vehicles, people or property and also compensates if the car is stolen or destroyed by fire, but policyholders pay for their own repairs. These policies are recommended for cheaper or older cars.

Comprehensive policies include payment for damage done to the insured car. Most drivers have comprehensive policies, with the best policies offering free hire cars when an insured car is being repaired. Insurers offer **no-claims discounts** of up to 70 per cent on premiums for drivers who have not made a claim for several years. These discounts can become so valuable that drivers pay for their own minor repairs rather than claim on a policy. For an extra premium drivers can protect or insure their no-claims bonus. Bonuses can be transferred from one insurer to another.

Drivers who shop around can halve their premiums with no loss of cover. The easiest way is to sample brokers, and direct and traditional insurers. Some drivers get better deals than others. Direct insurers keep claims bills and premiums low by being highly selective about who they insure. This is known as **'cherry picking'**. Many insurers refuse drivers aged 25 or under, or those with high-performance cars or poor driving records. Some drivers are refused cover because of their addresses or their jobs. But brokers say they can find suitable schemes for those given the cold shoulder by direct insurers and direct insurers have already started diversifying into these so-called non-standard risks.

There are other ways to cut insurance costs. Premiums will be cheaper if a car is kept in a driveway or garage or if it has an approved security system. Cutting the number of named drivers can also reduce premiums.

But insurers warn drivers not to lie when buying policies. Drivers paying reduced premiums after saying they do not use their cars for work may find insurers refusing to pay claims for cars stolen or damaged in their office car parks.

CHARITABLE GIVING

Many charities feared the National Lottery would hit their incomes. But 400,000 people between them gave £1bn to charity in the National Lottery's first year and the figure is not expected to fall. Donations can be made to work harder by forcing the government to join in the giving as follows:

Covenants
This is the most common route. Donors make monthly, quarterly or annual donations adding up to as little as £100 per year for at least four years. In response the government tops up the donation through basic-rate tax relief and the money is passed to the charity.

People can set up covenants by filling in forms from a charity. Higher-rate tax payers can reclaim a further 15 per cent of the value of their donations through their tax returns. They can either pocket the money or pass it on to the charity.

Gift Aid

This scheme was set up by the Inland Revenue to help people make lump-sum donations. These are grossed up by the Revenue. The minimum donation is £250. If it comes from a basic-rate taxpayer the charities get £330 in total. Higher-rate taxpayers can reclaim the difference.

Give-As-You-Earn

This involves making regular donations through a company-run scheme. Workers donate up to £75 a month or £900 a year. This money is taken from gross pay and passed on in full to the chosen charity. The plans can be changed or stopped at any time.

The charity account

This is run by the **Charities Aid Foundation**. People pay money in to the account and have donations grossed up by the taxman. In return they receive a cheque book and cheque card. These can only be used to give money to recognised charities and people can set up standing orders for regular donation.

One painless way to donate to a charity is to donate as you spend with a charity or affinity credit card (see section on credit and charge cards for more details).

CHARTISTS

These people try to predict future share-price movements by looking at historical data. Their crystal balls are charts which show trends in the prices of shares, bonds, commodities or market indices such as the FTSE 100 Index.

Share-price movements often seem to bear little resemblance to the state of the economy or to a company's financial prospects. Chartists say these swings are caused by changes in sentiment and result in investors trading en masse. Chartists try to predict these movements and buy before a bull market

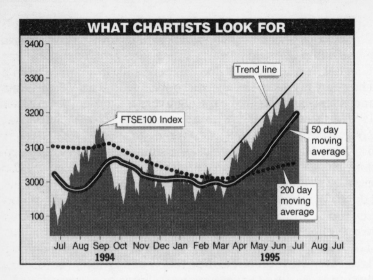

WHAT CHARTISTS LOOK FOR

Trend line

FTSE100 Index

50 day moving average

200 day moving average

Jul Aug Sep Oct Nov Dec Jan Feb Mar Apr May Jun Jul Aug Jul
1994 1995

takes off and sell before a bear market develops. The charts contain and process price data in different combinations.

The main tools of a chartist's trade are as follows:

- Recent and longer-term **moving averages**. These are plotted by totalling a company's share price over a certain period – say, 50 days – and dividing the result by the number of days involved.
- **Relative performance** against the stock market. This is calculated by dividing the share price by an index such as the Footsie and shows whether the share has outperformed, underperformed or performed in line with the index.
- Long-term **trends** in a share price. Trend lines are plotted by joining points on a share-price chart forming a straight line.
- **Head and shoulders** – no, not a brand of shampoo but an indicator intended to show the turning point of a market. If a share price graph resembles the outline of a human head and shoulders, this suggests shares are about to fall.

Conversely if a reverse head and shoulders formation develops (a head and shoulders upside down), this suggests shares could rise.

The chart opposite shows the Footsie during a recent period and its 50- and 200-day moving averages. From mid-August 1994 it showed the index traded in a range between 3,100 and 2,900, with a clear sideways trend. In mid-March 1995 it broke through the 3,100 level – a sign that buyers are beginning to outweigh sellers. More evidence is provided by the moving averages where they cut each other shortly after the Footsie breaks the 3,100 level. Both are moving upwards and the 50-day moving average cuts the 200-day moving average from below, forming what chartists call a **golden cross**. This shows both the short- and the long-term trends in the market have changed to an upward direction and is a key buy signal. Books on charting explain the theory in more detail.

CHILDREN'S SAVINGS

Children receive on average £4.14 in pocket money, and surveys show they are more thrifty than their parents. A recent survey revealed that they are three times more likely to save pocket money than the previous generation. There is an array of special saving schemes to help them do so.

Children pay tax if their earnings are high enough and 10,000 rich kids contribute to the Revenue's coffers each year. But child earners in the Macaulay Culkin or Shirley Temple league are rare and it is possible to ring-fence children's pocket money, gifts and other income from the Revenue.

Every child has a £3,765 income tax allowance – just like adults. They also have the usual £6,300 annual capital gains tax allowance. But many children are encouraged to place spare cash in savings accounts that pay interest net of tax instead of gross. This means £500m of needless tax is paid on children's savings every year. The answer is to register

Children are more thrifty than parents and are more likely to save pocket money than the previous generation

children's savings accounts for gross interest with the Revenue. This is done by completing the Revenue's **Form R85** when the account is opened. The same form can be used to reclaim tax already paid and is available at banks and building societies. The alternative is to put children's savings into a **National Savings** tax-free savings account.

The Children's Bonus Bond Issue H pays a tax-free 6.75 per cent for five years and needs a minimum deposit of £25. Each child can save up to £1,000 in the bond. After five years the bond can be repaid with interest, or rolled over for another five years. Other National Savings products suitable for children include the variable-rate investment account which needs a £20 minimum deposit. Deposits can be made at any post office. The 43rd Issue savings certificates which pay 5.35 per cent are also suitable.

Parents should be wary of making gifts to children that earn more than £100 of interest in a year. Anything earned above this will be added back when the Revenue calculates a parent's tax bill. Gifts from grandparents and other relatives and friends do not suffer this restriction. Other tax-free products such as Friendly Society bonds have been marketed to children but parents should be wary of high charges and poor performance on some policies.

Certain tax-free investments are not available to children – for example, Pep investors must be 18 or over. This does not stop parents or grandparents putting money aside for the long term for children through stock-market-based investments such as **unit trusts** and **investment trusts**. These can prove effective in building up a nest egg for children when they reach university age. An 18 or 21 year investment in an international growth or emerging market unit trust can provide high levels of growth but they are too risky and volatile for short-term savings. Invesco runs the **Rupert Bear Fund** which is targeted at people investing long term on behalf of children. The fund comes complete with Rupert Bear gifts if a big enough sum is invested and cards on a child's birthday.

COMMODITIES

Coffee, copper, gold, grain and oil are among commodities traded in London's financial markets. Brave investors can bet on whether prices are going to rise or fall. The three main commodities markets in London are:

1. **London Commodities Exchange**, which trades cocoa, coffee, white sugar, raw sugar, wheat, barley and potatoes.

This is expected to become part of the **London International Financial Futures and Options Exchange** later this year.
2. **London Metal Exchange**, which trades copper aluminium, lead, nickel, tin and zinc.
3. **International Petroleum Exchange**, which trades oil.

Producers use the exchanges to sell future production at pre-agreed prices, to reduce the risk of producing commodities when prices are healthy but selling them when prices have fallen. This is done through futures and options contracts. A futures contract allows a commodity producer to sell a commodity at a fixed price on a specified date. Buyers enter the market to satisfy raw material requirements if prices look like rising.

Speculators trade futures and options contracts before their expiry date and brave small investors can join them by becoming clients of a commodities broker. A list of private client brokers can be obtained from the exchanges. But novices should be wary: commodities are volatile and futures can massively magnify the risks involved.

However, private investors do not have to play the commodity markets. They can buy the shares of companies involved in or connected to these markets such as British Petroleum, British Gas, Ashanti Goldfields or RJB Mining, and they can also buy commodities trusts. Within the last two years investment houses such as Mercury Asset Management, Flemings, Barclays de Zoete Wedd and Hambros have launched commodities investment trusts or offshore-based vehicles. Commodity-based unit trusts have much longer track records although these tend to concentrate on oil or mining shares. A list of the managers of these funds can be obtained from the **Association of Unit Trusts and Investment Funds**.

COUNCIL TAX

This was born on April Fools' Day 1993 to replace the community charge or 'poll tax'. It is a local tax set by local councils to pay for local services. There is one bill per home whether this is a house, bungalow, flat, maisonette, mobile home or houseboat. The tax is levied on owned and rented property.

The size of the tax depends on the value of the home relative to other local homes. Valuations were carried out by an Inland Revenue division called the Valuation Office Agency and each home was placed in one of eight bands. Homes are listed according to their value on 1 April 1991 unless there have been any big changes since then such as an extension.

It is not possible to have a home moved into a lower council tax band as a result of general house price falls since 1991, but people can appeal on other grounds: for example, if part of a home has been demolished. Listing officers at local Valuation Office Agency branches can explain the banding and the appeals process.

Normally bills are issued in spring and paid in ten monthly instalments. There are four main ways of reducing these bills:

1. Discounts for homes in which there is just one adult.
2. Benefits for people on low incomes.
3. Reductions for some disabled people.
4. Transitional reductions for homes which would have faced a big rise in the shift from poll tax to council tax.

The **Department of the Environment** has leaflets on the council tax, advising how to appeal against it and how to claim a reduction. Copies are available from local councils, **Citizens Advice Bureaux** and the DoE at its Marsham Street headquarters in London (see useful numbers section at the back of the book).

CREDIT AND CHARGE CARDS

Britain has gone card crazy with record numbers of launches. Rates vary and so do the perks on offer. Customers with savings or current accounts with one bank or building society can go to any other for credit cards. Some cards give customers points for every £1 they spend and allow the points to be redeemed for gifts, money off new cars, flights, and even mortgages. Many cards charge annual fees of about £10 but several are free.

Choosing the right card depends on use. People who pay the full balance each month should apply for a fee-free card. They do not need to worry about interest rates. Those who borrow occasionally should check that the interest rate is competitive. People with big credit card debts should consider rival card companies. Many will take on existing debt, ring-fence it from new spending, and charge a lower rate of interest.

Charge cards such as American Express and Diners Club do not allow holders to borrow money. The full amount is paid off each month. The advantage is that they have no upper spending limits and charge-card companies have some of the best reward schemes for holders.

Storecards work like credit cards but can only be used in certain shops. There is rarely an annual fee, though interest rates can be higher. Holders are often given perks ranging from extra discounts to free clothes alterations. Those who agree to pay a minimum amount each month by direct debit are often charged a lower rate of interest.

With charity and affinity cards about £5 goes to a good cause when the card is taken out and about 25p is donated for every £100 spent. While individual donations are tiny, the money soon builds up. Affinity cards have donated nearly £10m to charities in ten years. Most charities and special interest groups, including political parties and universities, have cards. Banks rarely promote them, so people should go to charities for information.

Credit card insurance costs about £10 a year and means card details are held on a computer. If they are lost or stolen, insurers contact issuing card companies to organise replacements. Card companies can send customers details of their schemes.

D is for:

DEBIT CARDS

There are 26 million debit cards being used in the UK by people who increasingly find cash a bit of a bore, except for very small transactions, and who stopped using cheque books long ago for anything but their very biggest bills. If you throw in credit cards, then transactions using plastic, including debit cards, as opposed to cash grew by 25 per cent last year.

Indeed the cashless society is every banker's utopia, dispensing as it will with that bulky, inconvenient and costly commodity known as notes and coins. But the traditionalists among you need not worry. Although non-cash transactions are forecast to grow by 3 per cent a year, reaching 11 billion by 2000, there is still room among a naturally conservative financial public for the confidence and certainty bestowed by the feel of a crisp tenner.

Debit cards look like credit cards but in fact combine the role of cash and cheque book into one convenient plastic card. All the high-street banks offer the cards which are linked to one of two systems, **Switch** or **Vector**. The popularity of the cards has done much to convince some experts that the cashless society is nearer than we think.

The cards are swiped through terminals in shops and money is deducted from current accounts. They will only be accepted for payment if there is enough in the account to cover them. They can be used both at home and abroad in any shop, restaurant, theatre or other outlet that displays the relevant Switch or Vector logo. Most debit cards are called multi-use cards and can also be used to withdraw money from cash machines or to guarantee cheques.

But plastic card technology is moving fast and good old-fashioned debit cards are likely to be challenged in the near future by the next generation of cashless payment methods known as 'smart cards'. One of these is **Mondex** which works like an electronic wallet and has been piloted in Swindon. Instead of carrying a wallet containing cash people carry the Mondex card, which is electronically charged with a fixed amount of cash that can be used to buy items big or small. Once this amount of money is spent the card is empty and needs refilling. The card costs £1.50 a month. It can be loaded with money at a cash point or over the telephone using an identification number. The card can also be locked, again using the PIN number, to make it more secure than a normal wallet or purse.

But while competition to Mondex will be fierce, work is already well underway on providing people with a whole bank in their pocket, never mind just an electronic wallet. A specially developed mobile phone has been unveiled for credit-card users which will allow them to buy financial services, pay bills and view accounts at the press of a button.

All the figures show that paying by plastic is fast over-taking cash. The use of debit cards is forecast to double by 2000 to nearly two billion transactions and they have already surpassed credit cards as the most frequently used type of payment cards.

DENTAL INSURANCE

One of the first services to feel the sharp edge of the Conservative Party's strategic withdrawal from a universal welfare state was the six-monthly trip to the dentist. When most people received free dental treatment under the NHS, dental insurance did not exist. But they have proliferated now that NHS dentists are hard to find and basic check-up fees start at about £14. Five years ago 95 per cent of dentists offered a full NHS service. Today less than 60 per cent do so. Many people cannot find dentists prepared to take on new NHS patients and some dentists are automatically deregistering their NHS customers. The lucky few who are still being treated by an NHS dentist are likely to be paying 80 per cent of the cost of their treatment.

Despite all the pain, prices are rising fast. Silver fillings can cost up to £40 each, crowns can cost up to £300 and some complicated procedures can produce bills of more than £1,000. Insurance aims to spread the cost. Policies vary and are often advertised in dentists' waiting rooms or are available direct from insurers. Most policies cover check-ups, restorative work including fillings, crowns, bridges and sometimes dentures. But the small print may exclude some laboratory work for crowns and bridges which can reduce the insurer's bill. Most emergency treatment will be covered even abroad but most cosmetic treatments are rarely covered. Some insurers want customers' teeth assessed before offering a policy and charge premiums according to the dental report. Others take on all customers on equal terms and charge a premium according to the type of cover required. Monthly premiums start at £6 but can average £15.

DEPOSIT ACCOUNTS

The main form of savings vehicle offered by banks and building societies are deposit accounts. In general, the longer the money is tied up, the higher the interest rate offered, but consumers should be very cautious before committing money to a deposit account. The market for this form of saving is huge as is the range of rates on offer. People are advised to consider at least three or four deposit accounts before choosing one because the difference in return between the best and the worst comparable accounts can mean a saver missing out on hundreds of pounds.

Building societies tend to offer two types of accounts. First, **share accounts** give members voting rights and holders are treated as members of the society: they can participate in the way it is run and could qualify for bonus payments if the society is taken over, merged or converts to a bank.

Second, **deposit accounts** do not carry voting rights and holders are not treated as members of the society. Savers should check what they are getting before handing over their money.

The most accessible home for money and the deposit account with the lowest interest is the **instant access account**. These normally have minimum deposits of £1 and, in common with most savings accounts, pay tiered rates of interest so that the interest paid rises with the amount deposited.

Term or **notice accounts** state that withdrawals cannot be made without giving an agreed amount of notice, normally 30, 60 or 90 days. Some accounts will allow money to be taken on demand, but only after a penalty of, say, 90 days' interest has been deducted from the balance. Some of the newer notice accounts do allow holders to make one free withdrawal on demand each year.

Postal accounts are a recent arrival on the savings scene. As the name suggests all dealings must be by post, although leaflets describing how the accounts work are available in branches on request. Building societies say it costs less to run accounts by post from a central location and pass on the savings through higher interest rates. Some postal accounts claim to offer instant access but this tends to be by return of post.

There are some banks and building societies that offer extra interest to people who agree to make regular savings for a minimum of one year. People who have savings accounts at the same place as their current account should check to see if their savings are automatically swept into their current account if they go overdrawn.

Money in savings accounts is protected by a number of different safety nets. Savings with banks are covered by the **Deposit Protection Scheme** which covers 90 per cent of deposits up to £20,000. Building society money is protected by the Investor Protection Scheme which also pays 90 per cent of savings up to £20,000 if the society goes bust.

DERIVATIVES

'Welcome to the mad house', as any trader in the London derivatives market might say on a busy day. The young men and women who make their living trading derivatives have come to personify the fast-moving, high-pressure life of finance 1990s-style. With traders bedecked in garish jackets, howling and baying amid a flurry of incomprehensible hand signals, the modern derivatives markets are a far cry from the gentlemanly world of the old stock market.

As Nick Leeson might agree, some types of derivatives are high-risk investments promising roller-coaster rides of big potential returns and magnified losses. The collapse of Barings proved that derivatives can make fortunes and break banks. But they are not just for wealthy risk takers, and plenty of modest private investors use derivatives to reduce or **hedge** risks in their investment portfolio.

Derivatives are securities whose value depends on some other security or commodity. The basic ingredients are **futures** and **options**, and the latter are most suited to private investors. **Warrants** are also a form of derivative similar to options but are dealt with in more detail under the letter W.

Options are bets on the future price of anything from pork bellies and stock market indices to ordinary shares. More than 70 big British companies have options in their shares traded on the **London International Financial Futures and Options Exchange** (Liffe) and about 50 options brokers will act for private investors. Liffe will provide details of these firms and its number is listed at the back of the book.

Investors who buy options retain the right (but not the obligation) to buy or sell a share within a set time period at a price fixed at the outset. An investor may look at shares trading at 100p and feel they may rise quickly. Instead of buying the shares on the stock market and selling at a profit if they do rise, an investor could take out an option to buy at the **exercise price** of 100p at any time in the next three months. If the share price rises he or she can exercise the option and buy at 100p, which will be below market price. If it falls, the investor can allow the option to lapse, do nothing and lose just the **premium**, or **price** of the option, probably at about 15p a share.

This example above is of a **call** option where the investor has the right to buy in the set time period. On the other hand, investors who think shares might fall can take out a **put** option, which bestows the right to sell if the market moves as they predict. In effect, options give investors the right to buy or sell shares at a fraction of the market price.

When considering whether it is worth exercising an option investors have to look at the exercise price in comparison to the market price but also add on the price paid for the option. If an option is worth exercising it is said to be **in-the-money**. An option which would cost an investor the same to exercise as buying the shares in the market is said to be **at-the-money**, and an option which if exercised would result in a loss is said to be **out-of-the-money**.

Buying options is a low-risk way into the stock market; at worst, people stand to lose the price they have paid for the option. The opposite of buying options is to sell them, or **write** options as it is known in the market, and this can be extremely risky. Selling options imposes obligations but no rights whereas buying them bestows rights but no obligations.

A person who sells or writes a call must sell shares to the person who has bought the call option when it is exercised. This is bound to involve losing money for the option writer on what could be had from selling the shares into the stock market. Even worse is in store for people who write call options without owning the underlying shares. If the option is exercised they must go out and buy the shares in the stock market and then sell them for a lower price to the option holder.

Writing put options involves buying back shares from the put option holder who wants to sell the underlying shares. They must pay the put option holder the exercise price even though the market price of the underlying shares is sinking rapidly. **Futures** contracts are riskier because the investor has to exercise the option to buy or sell even if the market goes against him. Losses can be unlimited.

DIRECT DEBIT AND STANDING ORDERS

These two services do the same thing but in slightly different ways. They are promoted by banks as the easy, secure and hassle-free way of paying regular bills but unfortunately they have become one of the most common sources of customer outrage. The big banks have paid for TV advertising to promote direct debits which shows scores of relaxed and happy people secure in the knowledge that their regular bills are being paid. But ask direct debit customers who have been double charged what they think of the system and the answers are likely to be less favourable.

Direct debits allow the recipient of a regular payment – normally a mortgage, credit card, electricity or telephone company – to deduct the money when required. It can change the amount each time it demands a debit. Standing orders can be made out to the same organisations but the amount to be debited and the date it is to be taken from the account is set in advance and cannot be changed by the recipient. Standing orders keep the payer in control but are less flexible and less popular with recipients.

Many companies use incentives to encourage people to use direct debits, and some credit card companies charge a reduced rate of interest if customers agree to pay the minimum balance each month by direct debit. Other companies such as British Gas, British Telecom and the electricity suppliers cut their bill for people who pay by direct debit. Some mortgage lenders give better rates to borrowers with direct debits and many insurers discount premiums in the same way.

The problem with both direct debits and standing orders is that customers have to have enough money in their accounts to cover the deductions. If they do not, they face overdraft charges from their banks or building societies or late payment charges from the recipients or both. It is worth checking bank statements regularly to make sure that direct debits and standing orders are still relevant and correct.

The banks say the direct debit rules include a variety of safeguards to protect customers. These are as follows:

- If a company offering direct debits as a payment option wants to alter the payment date or amount it must give advance notice, normally 14 days.
- It must sign a refund guarantee so that bill payers are entitled to immediate funds if the wrong amounts are deducted.
- Payers must be allowed to cancel their direct debits at any time by contacting their banks.
- If there are any problems, people should contact their bank or building society.

DISCLOSURE

Hollywood made disclosure interesting by filming the Michael Crichton novel of the same name with Michael Douglas and Demi Moore in the starring roles. Disclosure in *Family Finance* is a little more mundane than the sexual politics, harassment and intrigue of the box office hit.

The new disclosure rules came into force on 1 January 1995 – D-Day, as it has become known. The rules force people selling insurance or pension policies to tell prospective investors how

Insurance or pension salesmen must reveal how much of the premiums will be eaten up in charges or other fees

much of their premiums will be eaten up in charges and fees. The information must be presented in clear language and on forms people can understand. In the past if this information was presented at all it was in the form of confusing percentages or reduction in yield figures. Now it has to be given in cash terms. The new regulations have made selling life and pension policies much more time consuming and difficult for the insurers.

The aim of disclosure is to help people shop around for the best-value policies before they buy. As before, advisers must say whether they are tied, selling the products of one insurer, or independent, looking through the marketplace for the most suitable deals (see under Advice for more detail). If people are buying regular premium policies both types of adviser must produce written records saying why the particular product has been recommended.

Consumers must also be given **key features documents** to explain what the policies are and how they work. They say what the product aims to do, how much the customer may pay, and how long the policy will last, and they specify the risks involved. Customers have to be given a key features document before they sign up for the policy and can change their minds if they do not like the look of the information provided.

Investors should check:

1. The amount of risk involved.
2. The amount the insurer will repay if the buyer surrenders the policy early. The figures given must be in cash terms and calculated according to the company's own charges rather than industry averages. Investors should be wary of products which repay very little on early surrenders.

E is for:

EMERGING MARKETS

Many investors think the biggest stock market returns of the future will not be made in London, New York or Tokyo but in cities such as Manila, Caracas, Lima and Mexico City.

The economies of these so-called emerging markets are expected to grow faster than those of their more mature counterparts. These countries combine low-cost, flexible workforces with a willingness to embrace new technology. They are also likely to be big spenders on capital projects to boost their standards of living, and governments are often involved in ambitious privatisation programmes as a way of developing their stock markets to encourage foreign investment. The result of these embryonic capitalist economies is the potential for high levels of economic growth coupled with large, if volatile, stock-market returns.

But the case for emerging markets has sadly been hijacked in recent years by the marketing and sales directors of investment houses, who have been pushing the idea of emerging markets as a panacea to satisfy the often unrealistic ambitions of private investors. In 1993 thousands were sucked into rising stock markets in Latin America and Asia as billions of dollars from around the world started chasing shares in emerging markets such as Thailand, Taiwan, Singapore, Mexico, Brazil,

India, Pakistan and even African stock markets such as Kenya and Nigeria.

Make no mistake, all these countries and more have encouraging long-term prospects. Nevertheless, anyone who invests in emerging markets needs to understand exactly what they are buying and the complex reasons why one minute the markets can be soaring and the next crashing, wiping out months or even years of gains in a few days.

The truth behind emerging markets is far more complex than the simplistic message of high, long-term growth prospects churned out by fund management groups. For a start, 1995 saw most established Western stock markets such as the United States outpacing the emerging markets. These were hit by a double whammy in 1994: first, in February by rising interest rates in the West, and secondly, by the Mexican currency crisis of December. This crisis sent the peso crashing, local interest rates soaring and the supposedly high-growth Mexican economy into recession. Even worse, it put other emerging stock markets around the world into a tail spin, giving the lie to a common emerging-market mantra that diversification across a range of stock markets will reduce much of the risk of these embryonic markets.

The emerging market bubble of 1993 was fuelled largely by US dollars washing out of America looking for a new and exciting home. But once the US central bank – the Federal Reserve – decided to raise interest rates to combat the threat of US inflation, the flow of this cash, or liquidity, dried up. In fact the money was repatriated back to the United States to take advantage of higher domestic interest rates. This highlights the fact that the fortunes of many emerging market currencies are closely linked to the US dollar. When American interest rates rise so too must those of the emerging markets to try to maintain economic stability.

The experiences of the last two years should have taught investors to treat emerging markets with much greater caution. But the setbacks in these new markets may present opportunities for investors willing to hop on the white-knuckle ride of the investment world and hang on for ten or twenty years. The investment industry in the City of London has, not surprisingly, made it easy for investors to buy into the golden story of emerging markets. People can choose between a host of unit trusts and investment trusts that pool investors' money together and buy a portfolio of shares in stock markets around the world. These vehicles are the best way for sophisticated savers to invest in emerging markets. Buying shares direct, while not impossible, is costly and even more risky than a well-spread portfolio available through pooled funds. Pension and life insurance policies also offer investors the chance to put some of their contributions in emerging markets.

The main emerging markets are either in the Far East or Latin America, though the ranks are being swelled by Eastern European countries and offshoots of the former Soviet Union that are slowly embracing capitalism and its trappings such as stock markets and shareholders.

Investors have three main choices of funds:

1. Global emerging market trusts that invest in a range of markets round the world and change the mix of these markets as the fund managers see fit.
2. Regional trusts that do the same but only for specific areas such as Latin America or the Far East.
3. Single country funds concentrated on one emerging stock market.

Funds in the last of these categories are the riskiest and are recommended only for those investors with cast-iron constitutions who already have a wide portfolio of general funds.

Emerging markets investment is for the long term. Analysts believe that these economies will take decades to mature, which makes them ideal for parents or grandparents putting money aside for children. But all investors have to be prepared to see the value of their funds fluctuate, as emerging markets are famously volatile, while advisers say that these markets are suitable homes for money that investors can afford to forget about for many years.

They also suit people wanting to invest small, regular amounts over the years to take advantage of pound cost averaging. By investing through the bad times as well as the good, investors will find themselves buying more units for the same amount of money when markets are low, producing better-than-expected lump sums if they sell when markets rise (see P for a detailed definition of pound cost averaging).

Returns from emerging markets have been impressive. Few unit trusts and investment trusts have got more than a five-year track record in this area, but even within this space of time investors can expect to have doubled their money and more in many instances. The average generalist emerging market investment trust over five years would have more than doubled your money, while the best one would have more than tripled an investment.

ENDOWMENTS

Few financial products have had as bad a press in recent years as endowments. They have been harshly criticised as expensive, inflexible and poorly performing investment plans that benefit the people selling them more than the buyers. But some of the censure has been overdone and many people find an endowment still suits their needs.

Most people who pay into endowment policies bought them to repay their mortgages. It is this group that bodies such as the Office of Fair Trading say have been the worst treated by commission-hungry salesmen eager to flog an endowment at any excuse. Endowment mortgages are packaged products sold by banks or building societies. Borrowers pay a monthly repayment that includes the interest on the loan, and a premium on a combined life insurance and investment plan.

The insurance element promises to repay the loan in full if the holder dies before the maturity date, while the investment element goes into the stock market aiming to build up a big enough fund to repay the loan at an agreed time, usually after 25 years. If the endowment fund grows faster than expected it will produce more than needed to repay the loan and the borrower can take the extra as a tax-free lump sum.

Endowments have been around for many decades and early investors have had their loans repaid in full and received more money on top. One of the criticisms about them has centred on the fact that today's lower-than-expected investment returns mean this cannot be guaranteed to happen in the future. Some endowment companies admit that existing plans may not even produce enough to repay holders' loans and are advising them to increase their monthly payments to boost returns.

The advantage of endowment policies is that they are designed to smooth out the peaks and troughs of stock-market movements. Investors start with a basic **sum assured** and have this increased each year by a series of **annual bonuses**. Once added, these bonuses cannot be removed even if markets crash. But fund managers do not pass on all the benefits of a market rally straight away. Some growth is held in reserve so that they can still pay bonuses in years when the stock market is flat or falling. Investors who stick with the endowment to its **maturity date** are paid a final or **terminal bonus** which can comprise up to 60 per cent of their total payment.

A problem with endowments is that investors are paid very little if they need to cash in their plans early. These **surrender values** have been rising recently, but most people would still be better off keeping up payments until their policies mature.

If this is impossible, investors have two options. The first is to make the endowment **paid up**. If this is done, the sum assured will be reduced, and future bonuses will be paid on the lower amount. The investor still benefits from a reduced amount of life cover and the endowment policy continues until maturity. The second choice is to sell or auction endowments on the **traded endowments market**. Several firms now act as intermediaries between buyers and sellers of policies. Sellers are likely to be paid up to 30 per cent more than the surrender values of their policies.

Buyers invest in other people's endowments for many reasons. Many like the fact that endowments smooth out investment returns over the years and buy them because they will produce a lump sum on a known date, helping to cover school fees, future tax bills or other expected payments. Some are buying because their own health is such that they do not qualify for the life insurance element of a new endowment.

The one thing people should remember about endowments is that they are contracts. You sign a contract to pay regular monthly premiums for an agreed number of years to the insurer, who invests the money for you and pays bonuses and a final maturity value. By surrendering the policy you are breaking the contract, which is why surrender values are so poor. True, this means endowments are less flexible than other investment vehicles such as unit trusts, which can be sold without penalty at any time. But endowments are also less risky. They are the only investment vehicle that provides such a wide spread of investments between shares, property and bonds, while smoothing out, through their bonus payments, the peaks and troughs that always occur with stock-market investment. And remember, once an endowment's annual bonus payment has been paid it cannot be taken away; it is guaranteed. Thus people are locking-in annual returns – an important advantage.

Investment returns are also healthy. Yes, endowment bonus rates have been doing more falling than rising in recent years, but so too have other stock-market-based investments during the early 1990s, and building society interest rates also rise as well as fall. After basic-rate tax, the average 25-year endowment is currently producing returns of 12.7 per cent a year, which is perfectly respectable.

ENTERPRISE INVESTMENT SCHEMES

These are high-risk investments offering tax breaks to 'business angels' – people prepared each tax year to put up to

£100,000 in a small unquoted business. EISs follow on from Business Expansion Schemes but offer less generous tax breaks at the outset.

Income tax relief at 20 per cent is given on the initial investment. This means it costs £8,000 to make an investment worth £10,000. Investors can also postpone paying capital gains tax on profits made elsewhere if this money is reinvested into an EIS. This means some investors may qualify for up to 60 per cent tax relief on their investments.

No capital gains tax is payable on EIS profits as long as shares are held for at least five years. The safest EISs have a **contracted exit,** a guaranteed minimum return on the initial investment. Unfortunately, contracted exit EISs are few and far between. Investors in standard EISs take big risks as there may not be a ready market in shares of unquoted companies when the time comes for the investment to be sold. As some consolation, if the EIS company fails, investors can offset their losses against other taxable income or capital gains.

Enterprise Zone Trusts are similar, though the risks can be greater and they have a poor and controversial track record. Income tax relief is given on the way in and investors can borrow the rest of their investment in the hope that the returns – normally rent on properties – will cover the interest. There is no maximum investment. Rents are guaranteed for between four and seven years. After that, investors will only get their money out if the EZT can find a buyer for the property. Problems will also arise if new tenants cannot be found when the guaranteed rental period ends or if the value of the property slumps.

ETHICAL INVESTMENTS

Investors have been 'going green' for years and as the chart on page 52 shows, the profits are building up.

Green and ethical investment was born in America where many investors are prepared to put their money where their

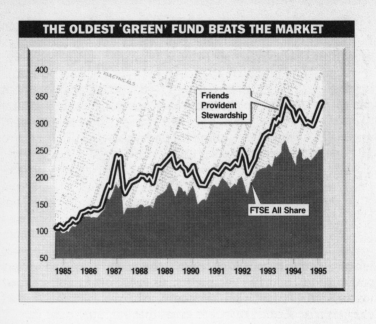

THE OLDEST 'GREEN' FUND BEATS THE MARKET

Friends Provident Stewardship

FTSE All Share

morals are. Investment funds are run according to a charter of ethical, environmental or moral guidelines. In the past the charters were dominated by lists of firms that investors would not buy into – normally those involved in animal testing, arms manufacture and so on. However, critics of ethical investment funds said these negative criteria imposed too many limitations on the fund managers and hit growth prospects.

The ethical funds hit back, emphasising a range of positive investment criteria which encouraged investment in companies involved in the manufacture and sale of environmentally friendly products. The idea is that these companies will grow faster in a world of consumers that are increasingly environmentally sensitive. This growth will be reflected in share prices and dividends. The list of acceptable investments for green fund managers is growing and some say they are prepared to invest in a third of companies in the FTSE All Share index.

Ethical funds are run according to charters of ethical, environmental or moral guidelines

Some unit trust ethical charters are more rigorous than others and this has a big effect on the underlying portfolio. Most exclude shares of tobacco companies, while some of the tougher charters also exclude shares of shops that sell cigarettes.

People wanting to invest ethically can buy into one of dozens of unit trusts or friendly society bonds. There are also several ethical Personal Equity Plans which allow people a guilt-free way of making tax-free money. At the same time, those who do not want to risk their money on stock markets can still find an environmentally friendly home: the Ecology Building Society and Co-operative Bank have ethical charters; the Co-op Bank will not lend money or offer accounts to companies involved in the activities shunned by the ethical fund managers; while Ecology also targets mortgage lending to environmentally friendly homes. Some independent financial advisers specialise in giving advice to people who want an ethical portfolio and their details are listed later in the book.

The **Ethical Investment Research Information Service** keeps an eye on how UK companies respond to ethical, environmental or social issues and advises many ethical fund managers how to check that their portfolios conform to their investment charters. EIRIS can also give investors a list of independent financial advisers who specialise in ethical trusts.

EUROPEAN MONETARY UNION (EMU)

No, not another alternative investment in large exotic birds but the Holy Grail of the financial world – European Monetary Union, otherwise known as the single currency. The current European Commission president, Jacques Santer, believes most European Union countries could join a single currency by 1999. Good news if you think our economic health depends on closer co-operation with our European neighbours, bad news if Europe means to you loss of sovereignty, interfering bureaucrats and economic and fiscal policy being dictated from across the English Channel.

True, a single currency for Europe inevitably means a single European central bank. This institution will be responsible for making sure that the value of the single currency is maintained, that is, protected against inflation. In order for it to work, however, this means **economic union** among the nations using the single currency.

The biggest supporter of a single currency is Germany. Its president, Roman Herzog, believes that without a single currency Europe will descend into the politics of the 1930s and will become a squabbling mass of states using such dubious competitive techniques as local currency devaluations to gain an upper hand in protectionist trade wars. In such circumstances, he foresees that countries such as Britain will follow self-interested economic policies which will lead inevitably to deflation and depression. As a brief résumé of what has gone on for most of this century, President Herzog's views are compelling.

His beliefs, and those of many other politicians from all over Europe including Britain, have succeeded in adding a new word to the English vocabulary – **Eurosceptic**. These people believe that a single European currency will serve well the interests of Germany and France but not Britain. It will reduce the competitiveness of British exporters compared to their European rivals who at present have to labour under the expensive franc and the Deutschmark compared to the relatively cheap pound and who have also signed up to the Social Chapter of the Maastricht Treaty – further adding to their costs. Significant decisions on interest rates and taxation will be taken away from Parliament and placed in the hands of faceless Eurocrats and undemocratic European institutions. But worse, say the Eurosceptics, is the political and social implications of a single currency.

The road to EMU has been a difficult one. The Maastricht Treaty, negotiated on behalf of Britain by John Major, lays down tough economic criteria for EMU membership related to things such as inflation, government borrowing and economic growth. In a bid to get all potential members travelling in the same direction the states of the European Union signed up to the **European Exchange Rate Mechanism (ERM)**. This fixed the value of everyone's currency against the Deutschmark but allowed some movement within certain bands. It was an obvious means of preparing for a future single currency. If a currency moved outside its permitted band governments were expected to take action, either by changing interest rates or trading their currency on the vast international foreign exchange markets.

Needless to say, the pound was perceived to be weak within the system and the Conservative government found itself both buying sterling and increasing interest rates to maintain the value of the pound. The first result of this was the longest and deepest British postwar recession. The second was a test of strength between Norman Lamont, then Chancellor of the Exchequer, and currency speculators such as **George Soros**. Not surprisingly George Soros won. He sold pounds, which he believed to be overvalued. To counter this selling Lamont had to raise interest rates to 15 per cent on Black Wednesday (16 September 1992), a position which was untenable, and the pound left the ERM, which itself subsequently collapsed the following August. A happy side effect for Britain of leaving the ERM was the ability to cut interest rates before anyone else, breathing life into the present economic recovery.

Despite this setback, monetary union is still high on the agenda of pro-European politicians, even though some countries may have to wait a while before joining. The big questions that European people must ask themselves is whether becoming a member of a European federation will rob them of their national identities and cultures and whether such changes as the social chapter of the Maastricht Treaty will add to the standards of living or reduce them by making their economies less competitive. The worry is that unless Western European nations co-operate more closely, the prospects for stabilising and integrating the powder keg which is Eastern Europe is much reduced.

$\mathcal{F}$ is for:

FINANCIAL SERVICES ACT 1986

This Act is a monumental piece of legislation that has spawned a huge bureaucracy in the name of consumer protection which many people, including some bureaucrats, believe has gone too far. It came into effect in April 1988 after a two-year gestation period. The architect of the legislation was **Professor Laurence Gower** (late of the Labour Party's commission on social justice) who was asked in the early 1980s to chair a committee on investor protection after an investment firm called **Norton Warburg** collapsed taking £8m of investors' money with it. It was Gower's proposals that enshrined in law the controversial idea of self-regulation for financial services companies.

Anyone who wants to carry on an investment business in the UK now has to be authorised under the terms of the Act. It also makes contravention of its rules and regulations a criminal offence, punishable by a maximum of seven years in gaol plus an unlimited fine. Sounds good, but the problem is that protecting the consumer from fraudsters, thieves and the incompetent is costing us a truly massive £330m a year, which is well above the amounts the Act has saved consumers by stamping out various abuses. Even when a really serious rogue is caught it is highly debatable whether or not the consumer receives justice, especially given the stiff punishments available to magistrates and judges by the Act. This particular problem was highlighted by the 180 hours of community service meted out to former independent financial adviser Roger Levitt, convicted of theft.

Originally the Whitehall department with ultimate responsibility for financial services was the Department of Trade and Industry. This later changed to the Treasury. But whoever has had responsibility for the area has faced controversy over the rising costs of regulation (paid for, of course, by consumers) versus the benefits received by those consumers. The FSA empowers the Treasury to regulate the investment industry. The Chancellor of the Exchequer is allowed to delegate his responsibilities to a designated agency, which in this case is the **Securities and Investments Board (SIB)**. The SIB, in turn, delegates some of its powers to subsidiary bodies known as **self-regulatory organisations (SROs)** and **Recognised Investment Exchanges (RIEs)**. Most private investors are concerned with the SROs. The Recognised Investment Exchanges are bodies such as the Stock Exchange and the London International Financial Futures and Options Exchange (Liffe). The SROs are as follows:

- **The Personal Investment Authority (PIA)**, responsible for policing all retail financial services except stockbroking. It covers the sale and marketing of financial products such as investments (units trusts, investment trust savings schemes), life assurance, pensions, and those who give financial advice. Its members include independent financial advisers, life assurance and pensions companies and investment firms. It resulted from a merger between two previous SROs, Fimbra and Lautro.
- **The Investment Management Regulatory Organisation (Imro)**, responsible for policing firms whose principal activity is investment management. Imro covers fund managers running unit trusts, pensions, life funds, and charities funds, as well as large private client accounts. It was the

SRO with responsibility for the monitoring of the Maxwell pension funds that were found to have been raided after Robert Maxwell's death.

- **The Securities and Futures Authority (SFA)**, responsible for firms dealing and arranging deals in securities such as shares, bonds, futures and options as well as giving advice on investment in these securities. The SFA is the regulator for stockbrokers and market makers in both the big institutional markets as well as the private client market.

FOREIGN CURRENCY

The world of foreign currency has two very different faces. One is the side holidaymakers see: small amounts of foreign currency bought and sold over the counter at travel agents, banks, building societies, post offices, *bureau de change* offices, airports and ports before they leave home. Then there is the international foreign exchange markets where currencies are bought and sold by governments and institutions such as banks, insurers, pension and investment funds to the tune of a staggering £562bn a day around the world.

For the humble holidaymaker the price of foreign money differs depending on where it is bought. Buyers should check both the exchange rate charged, which can change daily, and the commission or fee. Currency sellers offering the best rates may charge the highest fees, so both aspects have to be considered while shopping around. The exchange rate is often different for cash than it is for traveller's cheques.

Most high-street currency sellers have stocks of the main European coins and notes on hand at all times. Less common currencies normally have to be ordered and can provided within 24 hours. Currencies can normally be ordered by phone and some banks and building societies will deliver them for an extra fee. People do not have to have accounts with banks or building societies to use them to buy foreign currencies.

Some banks and building societies will deliver foreign currency for an extra fee

Most travellers should be wary of taking too much local currency – mainly because of the risk of theft, but also because holidaymakers normally have to pay more commission if they want to exchange it back into sterling when they return. One way to avoid these charges is to get currency from a company with a 'buy-back' promise – Travelex, the *bureau de change* operator at ports and airports, will exchange foreign currency back into sterling with no commission and at the rate it was originally bought. Some banks and building societies offer commission-free currency and traveller's cheques to gold credit card customers. They also allow free exchanges of unused currency back into sterling.

It is also possible to use cash machines to get local currency while abroad and currency is available from foreign bank branches. Most cashpoint cards are now part of international groups and can be used to withdraw local currency round the world. As these are not credit cards, users can only withdraw as much cash as their home accounts can stand. In some cases, there are no commission charges or fees for getting cash abroad but it is worth checking first. Note that obtaining currency over the counter in a foreign bank using a cashpoint, credit or charge card will be more expensive than buying it with cash at home. Credit or charge cards are particularly expensive as any local currency taken through one is treated as a cash advance and is subject to interest immediately.

The other aspect of the foreign exchange world is made up of the global foreign exchange markets. Latest figures from the Bank for International Settlements show that the amount of currency bought and sold in a typical day in London is a mind-boggling £300bn, compared with £158bn in New York and £104bn in Tokyo. This is trading on a grand scale, often by governments to protect the value of their own currencies, and by banks on behalf of their corporate clients, which have to do business all over the world and so need plenty of foreign cash. Insurers and pension fund managers who control billions of pounds of assets are also big players. Then there are the speculators, traders who buy and sell currencies to make multimillion pound profits every day from the tiny margins they earn when trading huge sums. It was on the foreign exchange markets that speculators such as hedge fund manager **George Soros** broke the Bank of England on Black Wednesday in 1992, which forced Britain out of the European Exchange Rate Mechanism.

The foreign exchange dealers (FX dealers in the technical parlance) who man the trading floors and make the markets work are the epitome of the modern City of London. At work by 7 a.m., having typically driven in by a black Porsche 928, a dealer at a top London FX bank will earn £40,000 a year two years after joining plus a 50 or 60 per cent bonus in a good year. The upper limit is between £100,000 and £125,000 for a chief dealer plus a 100 per cent bonus in a good year.

FRIENDLY SOCIETIES

The first friendly societies were formed more than 200 years ago and many are still going strong today. The early societies – with names such as the Ancient Order of Druids, Woodcutters and Woodmen – were the forerunners of modern insurers and building societies, and are still run as mutuals and effectively owned by their customers.

Some of the modern societies now sell everything from pensions to Personal Equity Plans, but their most popular products remain tax-free regular savings schemes. Investors pay a maximum of £25 per month, or £270 a year, for a minimum of ten years to qualify for the tax break. Friendly societies invest this money in building society accounts or shares, and returns are free of both income and capital gains tax. However, investors lose out if they have to cash in plans before the ten-year term is up and may not even get back the premiums they have paid in.

Some societies allow investors to pay their full ten years of premiums up front. The money is put on deposit and drip-fed into the tax-exempt bond over the years. Many advisers recommend tax-exempt bonds simply because they are a useful tax break for people who already have Personal Equity Plans and Tessas and want to keep more of their money out of the tax net. But there are problems. Plan charges are high and past performance has not always been sparkling. In the past, up to 60 per cent of the first year's premiums were taken in charges, along with hefty monthly fees. The societies say they were forced to charge so much because the low maximum investment limits meant they were unable to earn economies of scale on their operations.

Several have cut charges since the maximum investment was increased to £25 a month recently, and all are trying to boost the performance on their funds. New investors get the best deals, but existing savers are slowly seeing their policy terms improved, often by a slight cut in monthly fees.

Since 1991 it has been possible to take out tax-exempt policies on behalf of children, though each child can only have one plan and not every society sells children's bonds. Some friendly societies have also branched out into green investments and offer ethical funds as well as their normal ones, while the most active friendly societies are considering setting up long-term care or nursing home fee insurance policies and offer discount general insurance policies. More information about the friendly society movement can be obtained from the National Conference of Friendly Societies.

FUND MANAGERS

Fund management companies such as M & G, Perpetual and Prudential employ individual managers to run pension, investment, insurance, unit or investment trust portfolios.

Management companies normally offer a full range of funds investing in different types of shares and other instruments around the world. Each fund will probably be run by a different manager who is given strict briefs – to concentrate on UK blue-chip shares, European smaller companies shares or Latin American shares, for example. Because of this, fund management groups may not produce great results in every sector and some are famous for, say, Far Eastern investments, while others have better track records on European funds.

Individual fund managers run portfolios according to set goals, so some funds aim to achieve capital growth while others aim for high income. Most individual fund managers are big stock market players and some are in charge of portfolios worth hundreds of millions of pounds. Individual fund managers are backed by teams of researchers and assistants and follow leads from in-house or external stockbrokers. Many managers travel widely to visit the companies they invest in.

Some successful managers have built up strong reputations as leaders in their investment fields and have a large number of fans among private investors. Individual fund managers are sometimes poached between fund management groups and the cult of personality is such that some investors switch their investments and follow individual managers between companies.

Not all individual fund managers are human. Index-tracking funds, born in America and gaining popularity in Britain, use computers to replicate various stock market indices. The computers say how many shares in each company have to be bought to match the index. Index funds only trade when the constituent parts of the index change, so they are often cheaper to run and charge less than actively managed rivals.

Some banks, building societies and other players do not have in-house fund managers for the own-label investments they offer to customers, but instead contract out funds to existing fund management groups – Virgin Direct, for example, employs Norwich Union to manage its index-tracking fund. Before starting any investment it is worth checking who will be managing the money and looking at their track records.

FUNERAL PLANS

It is said that two things in life are certain: one is taxation, and the other is death. Tax is dealt with elsewhere in this book. Apart from the obvious suffering that death causes to families and friends it has one other sting in its tail and that is cost. **Inheritance tax** or the lack of a **will** can both prove costly to those left behind, as can a funeral.

Prepaid funeral plans are designed to cover this latter cost and were first offered in Britain in the 1980s, after selling well in Australia, Canada and the United States. The theory behind the plans is simple. People pay a lump sum or a series of monthly payments now, on the understanding that whenever they die their funeral will be paid for in full by the prepaid plan company.

But why bother with such a policy which you yourself will never benefit from? Is it just another cleverly packaged but largely unnecessary policy from the insurance industry? The truth about funerals is that they are expensive and getting dearer all the time. The reason, like most things these days, is a matter of economics. The country is fast running out of cemetery space. Demand is outstripping supply and the government is under pressure to change the law to allow the re-use of existing graves to alleviate the shortage.

Some inner-city councils have officially run out of burial space and are sending people to neighbouring boroughs in the hope of finding spare plots. But local authorities will normally levy a surcharge on people from other boroughs who want to use their burial services, further increasing costs. At the same time the government has announced plans to cut the amount of state aid given to low-income families faced with paying for a funeral.

The cost of a funeral can range from £890 to £3,095 with coffins ranging in price from £128 to £2,333. The average cost of a basic funeral is now more than £1,000. These costs have two elements:

1. Fees charged by the funeral directors.
2. Disbursement costs such as church services, cemetery fees and cremation fees.

With a prepaid funeral plan customers can give the insurer full details of every aspect of the funeral they would like, including hymns to be sung and readings, to ensure that relatives or friends will not have to make these decisions in times of grief. Such 'pay now, die later' schemes are becoming more popular and are offered by several companies and backed by many charities. The plans can make economic sense. Funeral costs are rising by more than the rate of inflation. Prepaid plans allow people to pay a fixed amount in today's money and plan-holders are promised their funerals will be paid for whenever they die, regardless of how fast prices have risen in the meantime.

The younger people are when they take out plans, the more they stand to save and some prepaid-plan companies have customers in their early twenties. People are normally promised guaranteed acceptance and do not have to take medicals before being offered a plan. There is no upper age limit for applications.

Prices start at about £800 and most plans offer a range of funerals from standard to de luxe. They also allow customers to pay in monthly instalments for up to five years. If customers die before the total costs have been paid, the remaining charges will be deducted from their estates. The plan companies invest premiums to make big enough returns to cover the rising cost of funerals.

But there are problems. The Office of Fair Trading was sufficiently worried to step in and investigate the business in 1995. It concluded that the prepaid funeral industry could be worth £500m by 2000 but in the absence of any regulation people, often in their seventies, had to rely on the honesty and competence of providers to safeguard their investment. The OFT director-general said there was serious potential for fraud, mismanagement and overselling and that consumers faced considerable risk from rogue players. The OFT also points to the marketing and selling practices used by some of the companies, particularly the payment of incentives to charities to endorse plans and the sales presentations being made in nursing homes and residential homes. The Department of Trade and Industry is still considering the OFT's report.

Two prepaid funeral plan companies have already been forced into liquidation with insufficient assets to provide the funerals for which people have paid. Thus there are several points people should check before taking out a prepaid funeral plan:

1. Are all payments put straight into an independent trust fund separate from the plan company?
2. Is there a guarantee that the plan-holder, their family or estate will not have to pay any more money in the future, regardless of the rising cost of funerals?
3. Does the plan cover all extra charges or disbursements to funeral staff?

Some people may also want to opt for a company that allows them to choose a named funeral director or funeral company rather than relying on one chosen by the prepaid plan company. People who plan to retire abroad should also check what will happen if they die overseas.

G is for:

GAZUMPING

This was one of the worst aspects of the 1980s housing boom – and some estate agents say it is starting to rear its head again in the 1990s.

It happens when someone selling a house agrees a price with a potential buyer who gets a survey done and arranges a mortgage. The buyer is ready to complete the deal when the seller gets a better offer for the house, accepts this higher price and leaves the first buyer out in the cold. That buyer, who has paid for the survey and possibly paid an application or booking fee for a mortgage, has been gazumped.

The law in England and Wales allows gazumping, since verbal or even written agreements made before the exchange of contracts are not binding on either party.

Estate agents say gazumping is back because there is a shortage of decent houses for sale. Many people are delaying putting their houses on the market in the hope that prices may start rising soon. So the good houses that are available are in demand from several buyers, and sellers are able to play one off against another.

But sellers can be victims as well as villains. Buyers can be guilty of **gazundering**, when they agree a price with the seller, proceed with the sale up until exchange of contracts when all

The buyer is ready to complete but the seller gets a better offer, accepts it and leaves the first buyer out in the cold

other potential buyers have lost interest, and then reduce the price they are prepared to pay for the house. If the sellers are desperate to move and do not have time to seek other buyers, they may have to accept the lower offer.

The rules are different in Scotland where letters or **missives** between buyers and sellers form binding contracts. The **conclusion of missives,** when a price is agreed between two parties, is a written deal which cannot be altered. In Northern Ireland, however, houses are bought and sold according to the systems in England and Wales so gazumping and gazundering can be rife.

GILT-EDGED SECURITIES

These are fixed interest bonds issued by the government as a way of borrowing money. They pay investors a fixed level of interest over a number of years and with most dated gilts the government redeems them at their face value at the **maturity date.** Income is paid in two six-monthly instalments.

Gilts are seen as one of the least risky ways of investing because they are fully backed by the government. Barring a big national catastrophe, investors know they will always receive their income and that gilts will be redeemed in full. Gilts are issued with a range of maturity dates so investors can buy them to meet specific requirements in the future. Many people use them to provide extra income in retirement and they are also popular to help pay for future school fees.

Gilts that mature within five years are called **shorts,** those maturing between five and 15 years are called **mediums,** while those due to mature 15 years after issue are called **longs.** Some gilts are issued without maturity dates and are called **undated gilts.** The government can redeem these at any time, though it may never do so – War Loan has been trading since 1915. Other gilts are given two dates between which they can be redeemed.

A few gilts are issued with variable rates of interest and are known as **floating rate gilts.** The interest on these falls and rises in line with interest rates in the money markets. Other gilts have their returns linked to inflation. Both interest and

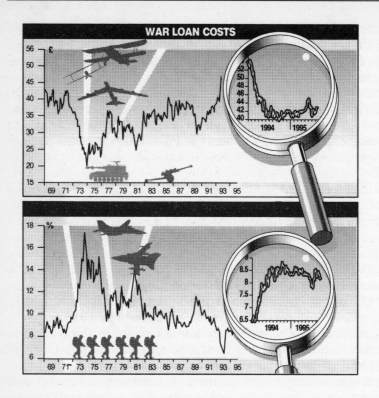

WAR LOAN COSTS

The graphs show the volatility of gilt-edged securities prices and the need for investors to get the timing right when they trade.

Both show the performance of the 3·5 per cent War Loan, the undated gilt launched in 1915 to help pay for the First World War. It has been savaged by inflation and has had a controversial history.

The upper graph shows how the price has fluctuated since 1969 while the lower graph shows the oscillations in its yield.

An investor who bought at the bottom of the bear market at the end of 1974 when £100 nominal of the stock cost about £20 would have an income of more than 17 per cent. Today he would also have doubled his capital value.

By contrast, an investor buying at the top of the 1993–94 bull market in bonds would have paid £54·41, would have a 6·4 per cent income and would now be sitting on a capital loss of more than £11.

capital growth vary with the level of prices and these gilts are called **index linked**.

The government issues gilts through the Bank of England which holds regular **gilt auctions**. These are used mainly by institutional investors to buy gilts for their investment funds, though the Treasury is trying to encourage more private investors to apply for gilts through the auctions and advertises them widely in advance. Despite the growing popularity of auctions, most private investors use a **stockbroker** to buy them or invest through **National Savings** which can be done with forms from main post offices. Investors should ask for copies of the free information leaflet, *Government Stock*, which explains what gilts are, who should use them and how to buy them.

Stockbrokers typically charge 1 per cent for the first £10,000 of gilts bought and 0.4 per cent thereafter, which includes the cost of any advice on which gilts are most suitable. National Savings charge 0.6 per cent for the first £5,000 and then 0.35 per cent but no advice is given.

Another way to invest is to buy a gilts-based **unit trust**. The trust is managed by a fund manager who pools together private investors' money and invests it in a portfolio of different gilts and other bonds issued by foreign governments and some large companies. Unit trusts allow small investors to spread their risks by investing in a wide range of gilts rather than concentrating on just one or two issues. It leaves the decision of which gilt to buy to a professional fund manager, which makes things easier for private investors. Gilts are also held by unit trusts that qualify for the tax-free status of **Personal Equity Plans**. The new generation of corporate bond Peps can hold a proportion of their assets in gilts with the rest invested in bonds issued by companies.

Once the Bank of England has auctioned a new issue of gilts they are then listed on the stock market and can be bought and sold in the normal way. This is when most private investors buy. But although gilts are seen as low-risk investments, they do carry risks.

A recent gilts issue was the Treasury 8.5 per cent 2005. For every £100 invested at auction the government will pay £8.50 per year income and repay £100 in 2005. The fixed rate of interest is called the **coupon**. But the price of these gilts may have risen since they were listed on the stock market. Instead of paying £100 to get £8.50 of income, investors must now pay £103. This means the level of income, or yield, provided by the gilt has fallen from the original 8.5 per cent to 8.25 per cent. Investors are also locking themselves into a guaranteed capital loss by paying £103 for a gilt which will be redeemed at £100 on the maturity date.

Gilt prices can also prove volatile. Between the beginning of February 1995 and February 1996 the Treasury 8.5 per cent 2005 price has fluctuated between a low of £97 and a high of £108. The price of gilts is hit by two main factors: interest rates and inflation. If the Chancellor of the Exchequer decides to raise interest rates the fixed returns of gilts become less attractive, while the variable rates paid on savings accounts look more tempting as they tend to rise in line with base rates. The price of gilts will fall as a result. If interest rates fall the opposite is true. The fixed returns of gilts are a better deal when savings rates are falling so gilt prices rise. Rising inflation, or the expectation of rising inflation, will have a similar effect to rising interest rates. The fixed returns available on gilts are eroded as the cost of living rises, so their prices fall. If inflation is falling, then the real returns from gilts increase and gilt prices rise.

Prices proved particularly volatile recently after the government announced big changes to the way gilts are taxed. From April 1995, capital gains made from gilts will be liable to tax for the first time and investors will have to pay income tax on their gains. The government originally planned an exemption level of £20,000 but raised this to £200,000 after investors protested. This means a married couple can hold £400,000 of gilts and escape tax on any gains. Holders of two low-coupon gilts popular with private investors (Funding 3.5 per cent 1999/2004 and Treasury 5.5 per cent 2008/12) will also be exempt from the new tax regime.

GUARANTEED GROWTH BONDS

These are a relatively new type of investment that tries to combine the generally superior returns of stock-market-based investments with the security of a deposit account.

For a minimum investment – normally £5,000 – investors are guaranteed a minimum return plus the prospect of extra growth if the stock market rises. If the stock market falls over the life of the bond, investors know they will get back at least their original stake. One big drawback to the bonds is that investors do not benefit from dividends paid out by companies as the returns are based only on the stock market's capital growth. Dividends have formed an important part of investors' returns from the stock market in the past.

The bonds also require people to lock their money away for a number of years to qualify for the guarantees. A typical life for the bonds is five years and investors face big penalties if they want to withdraw their money early.

The level of protection against stock market movements varies. Some bonds promise to repay original capital plus 30 per cent after five years regardless of how the stock market performs. This is equivalent to 4.9 per cent growth per year. Others simply promise to repay original capital.

Investors should also look at the amount of growth they get from stock-market rises. This also varies widely between bonds. Some will add 100 per cent of any stock-market return, as measured by the FTSE 100 Index, to 100 per cent of investors' capital. Others will apply only 50 per cent of stock-market growth to just 96 per cent of investors' capital. Some pay more than 100 per cent of stock-market growth.

Another problem is that some bonds will limit the total growth available so that investors' gains are capped even though the stock market might continue to grow. The bonds invest in complex stock-market-linked securities called **derivatives** to achieve their performance. Some bonds average out the returns achieved in the last year and add that to the final return. This means that if the stock market should crash just before the bond matures, investors can still receive a positive return. A number of the bonds also **lock in** gains at regular intervals, which means investors will benefit from past gains even though the stock market might be falling at maturity. The only way to shop around is to ask for actual figures to indicate how much the bond will be worth if the stock market grows by different amounts in the time period.

Some of the companies that buy and sell second-hand endowment policies now trade in guaranteed bonds, offering an escape route for investors who want to sell before the maturity dates. Guaranteed Peps hit the headlines with the launch of corporate bond Peps this summer. Legal & General and Johnson Fry have launched corporate bond Peps that invest in a single bond and offer investors guaranteed returns. But investment advisers warn investors to remember that everything has a price, and the price of a guarantee normally comes through higher charges or lower yields.

Several pension companies and independent financial advisers offer guaranteed pension funds that lock in stock-market gains. Some recommend that people close to retirement move their money out of a pure equity fund into a guaranteed fund to cut their risks. Most work in a similar way to guaranteed growth bonds by offering a percentage of growth in a chosen stock market index in return for an assurance that the fund value will not drop if markets fall.

GUARANTEED INCOME BONDS

These provide risk-averse investors with a safe, fixed level of income and with a promise to repay original capital on maturity. The bonds are offered by insurers and building societies which invest in fixed interest securities issued by big companies such as British Gas and British Telecom as well as gilt-edged securities.

Guaranteed income bonds pay interest annually, net of basic-rate tax. Many will pay investors monthly but at a slightly lower rate than for annual payments. Minimum investments range from £1,000 to £100,000 but investors should shop around for the best deal. A £3,000 investment with one insurance company over five years will pay 6 per cent while £3,000 in another company's bond pays just 5 per cent over the same period.

Investors buy guaranteed income bonds mainly for the fixed levels of income they provide. This is attractive to investors who fear a fall in interest rates. The certainty of regular income is also attractive to people trying to manage a tight budget. The bonds can also be used for capital growth by reinvesting the income over the investment's life.

The bonds are also covered by the Policyholders Protection Act should one of the insurers collapse. This will repay 90 per cent of an investor's capital and has no maximum payout. Depositors in building societies are covered by a protection scheme which also pays out 90 per cent of capital but has a maximum award of £18,000.

Independent financial advisers can help investors shop around for the best deals.

$\mathcal{H}$ is for:

HEALTH INSURANCE

These policies are designed to pay out a lump sum or regular, monthly income to people unable to work because of illness or injury. Lump-sum payments are made by **critical illness** or **dread disease** policies while regular income is paid by **permanent health insurance**. It is worth getting cover. Most people in Britain are insured against the financial consequences of theft or death but relatively few are covered against the impact of illness, which could dramatically reduce household income.

Instead, most people still rely on the state, and a recent survey showed that 72 per cent of people thought the government should replace income lost through an illness lasting six months or more. But the government is cutting back on the help it gives. In April 1995 a new invalidity benefit was introduced. This only pays out if a person is unable to carry out any job due to illness or injury. Previously it had paid benefit to people who were simply unable to do their own job. As a result, about 750,000 people will miss out on state benefit. The government also used to reimburse 80 per cent of short-term sickness pay made by employers but this has now been cut.

Employers are also unlikely to afford long-term sickness pay as few have group policies, especially smaller companies.

This is where critical illness and PHI policies come in. **Critical illness policies** pay out a single lump sum if the plan-holder suffers a heart attack, stroke, cancer, kidney failure, major organ transplant, coronary artery bypass surgery, total permanent disability, or one or other of a long list of medical conditions. Policies pay up even if the policyholder is able to continue to work after diagnosis.

The statistics showing the risk of suffering critical illnesses are grim. Each year 150,000 people have their first heart attack and half are alive one year later. In fact people are three times more likely to suffer a critical illness and survive than they are to die, but there are seven times more life assurance policies in force than critical illness policies.

Permanent health insurance policies pay a regular income instead of a lump sum in the event of illness or disability – most insurers offer policies. The conditions covered vary from contract to contract but range from loss of a limb in a car accident to long-term illnesses such as multiple sclerosis, ME, or a back problem. Potential policyholders should check what type of cover is available. Some PHI contracts will pay out if a person is unable to do their own job while others will only pay out if a person is unable to do any job. It is also important to choose a contract which covers a wide range of conditions. Applicants will be asked about their previous medical history when insurers are setting premiums.

The policies are barred by the government from paying out more than 75 per cent of a person's net monthly earnings. But they will pay out indefinitely. The word 'permanent' means monthly payments will be made from the start of an illness to normal retirement age as long as the policyholder remains unable to work. So a man aged 30 who is unable ever to work again should get 35 years of payments, even if he has only been paying premiums for a short time.

The cost of a PHI policy reflects an occupation's riskiness. A policeman is likely to pay higher premiums than an office clerk because of the greater risk of injury. For a professional male £500 per month of benefit would cost about £16 per month premium; for a woman it would cost £19. For a manual worker the same cover would cost £41 per month for a man and £46 per month for a woman.

HEDGE FUNDS

Despite their name, hedge funds have nothing to do with low-risk investment or 'hedging your bets'. Risks are high and they are aimed at rich individuals and big institutions. Most are based offshore in tax havens such as Bermuda in order to escape financial regulation.

There is a good reason for this. The regulators of the main financial markets in the United States, Japan and Europe are extremely worried about hedge funds and the fact that the activities of hedge funds can make their supposedly solid financial systems look extremely weak and vulnerable. Regulators from these countries would dearly love to control hedge funds and cancel out the threat they pose. The potency of the hedge funds comes from their sheer size and the highly speculative nature of what they do.

At its simplest, hedge fund managers make bets. But they bet with billions of dollars at a time and they use the world's financial markets as their casino. As a result, the activities of a few big hedge funds run by a handful of people can move markets dramatically one way and then another. Recent examples of this occurred in the silver and crude oil markets.

Hedge fund managers offer clients the prospect of big profits that outperform other investments. To deliver these promises they need to take big risks. One way is to borrow money to boost their exposure to financial markets. This is known as **gearing** or **leverage**. This has been another big cause for concern among financial regulators who worry that some big banks are lending too much to these high-risk betting machines. The regulators' worst nightmare is something called **systemic risk**. This might involve a hedge fund borrowing large sums from a particular bank or banks and then losing it all on a particularly bad financial bet. It cannot repay the banks, which are forced into losses and unable to meet their own liabilities to other clients. In turn, this creates a domino effect of financial collapses throughout the system, hence the term 'systemic risk'. Small wonder, then, that banks are being told by their central bank regulators to carefully monitor their lines of credit to these funds and not become overexposed.

Hedge fund managers are paid by performance-related fees. They often take up to 20 per cent of profits as fees – another reason to go for big returns – plus a 1 to 2 per cent annual management charge. The funds usually demand minimum investments of between $500,000 to $10m and require investors to commit funds for at least a year. The funds first appeared in the 1940s but did not really take off until after the 1987 crash. About 800 hedge funds now exist with up to $100bn under management. Many of the trades made by hedge fund managers are big bets on the direction that currencies, bonds and share prices might take.

The most famous hedge fund gamble was made by **George Soros** – the man who 'broke the Bank of England'. He made investors in his Quantum hedge fund nearly $1bn by selling pounds when sterling crashed out of the **ERM** in September 1992, despite the efforts of the Bank of England to support the currency. This is the kind of havoc that hedge funds can wreak or at least contribute to significantly. Soros exposed those famous 'fault lines' that John Major spoke of within the ERM – Soros would have called them 'inefficiencies', and where there are inefficiencies, even on the grand scale of a nation's currency, there is money to be made. In this case, Soros and his hedge fund went **short** on sterling. This means he sold pounds on the foreign exchanges with the intention of buying them back at a later date when they were worth less.

Going **long** means buying an asset with the intention of selling it in the future. Going long or short are typical hedge fund bets. The tactic does not require fund managers to physically own the assets involved. Soros sold sterling **futures**

contracts instead. These allowed him to agree a sale but receive payment in three months' time at a fixed price. When the futures contract matured Soros received the pre-agreed fixed price but was able to make a huge profit by buying back pounds, which had by then fallen in value.

But when hedge fund managers get their bets wrong the results spell disaster. In February 1994 a rise in US interest rates sent markets into a spin, hitting hedge funds with huge losses. Soros admitted losing $600m alone in one gamble on the dollar/yen exchange rate on 14 February 1994 – an event in financial circles that was given the inevitable 'massacre' tag. Bond and stock markets fell in unison as a wave of selling overtook investors. A big problem for hedge funds when markets start to fall is their sheer size. In order to make money the funds need to be flexible and be able to switch in and out of market quickly. But with $2bn under management in just one fund, being nimble becomes almost impossible – once again increasing the risks.

More recently the activities of hedge funds have been more subdued and the regulators' fear of the funds has subsided a little. After becoming the whipping boys for everything that went wrong in financial markets the funds are once more becoming acceptable. After big gains in 1992 and 1993 hedge funds were hit by sharply falling bond and share prices in 1994 after US interest rates started to rise. Investors started to withdraw their cash as a result. This slimming down of the funds was encouraged by the managers themselves who started to hand back cash to investors, reducing the size of the funds and making them more manageable as a result.

HOME INCOME PLANS

These allow older home owners to use the value of their houses to boost their monthly incomes. Home owners sign away part or all of their houses to a plan company but retain the right to live in them rent-free for the rest of their lives, during which time they are paid monthly incomes. Thousands of people say decent home income plans have helped them enjoy their retirement to the full – but the schemes have had a controversial history. More than 2,000 elderly people have been ruined by high-risk home income plans taken out in the 1980s and have received £30m compensation as a result of being misled about the prospects for their schemes.

These controversial home income plans were called investment-backed plans. They involved the proceeds of a mortgage being invested in the stock market and plan-holders being told that the income from the investments would easily outstrip the interest payments on the mortgage. This did not happen and many people lost both their homes and their life savings in the ensuing debacle. The victims of home income plans went to the House of Lords in 1995 to try and get their compensation increased. The original level of compensation was fixed by the board of the **Investors Compensation Scheme** (ICS). It decided compensation would not cover money that had been taken from the original loans and spent. But the unhappy investors argued that compensation should be related to the entire loans because they would not have spent the money if they had been properly advised by the people whose businesses are supposed to fall within the remit of the ICS. They further argued that the ICS should not be allowed to use its discretion when setting compensation but that the amounts paid should be decided by a court in line with legal precedents.

Obviously this had big implications for any future compensation payments made for whatever reason. A judicial review threw out the investors' claims but a subsequent Court of Appeal judgment overturned that decision and said that compensation should cover the whole mortgage and that the ICS did not have discretion when setting compensation levels. In the end the House of Lords rejected the Court of Appeal's decision, ruling instead that the existing compensation paid to home income plan victims was adequate.

In a bid to recover the money paid out in compensation, the ICS then issued writs itself against building societies that had provided the mortgages involved in the investment-backed home income plans. The ICS claimed that societies such as the **Cheltenham & Gloucester,** now part of **Lloyds Bank,** owed a duty of care to investors to ensure that the home income plans they bought were financially sound and prudent, and that they should have warned customers of the risks to which they were exposed in entering the schemes.

Indeed the saga of home income plans continues. The ICS says complaints about failed schemes continues to be the most common subject of claims. Investment-backed home income plans have been outlawed and a new generation of safe home income plans has been created with no risk to users. There are two types of safe plan and both require people to have homes valued by independent surveyors.

Home reversion schemes
These tend to be recommend to people with properties worth more than £75,000. Owners agree to sell all or a proportion of a house to a safe home income plan company and are given a lump sum or a regular income for life in return. If only a percentage of a house has been given up then the remainder is left for owners to give away in their wills. They can benefit from any house price inflation along the way and can sell more slices if they need to raise extra money.

Mortgage annuity plans
These involve a fixed-rate home loan of up to £30,000 being taken out on a property. The money raised buys a fixed-rate annuity that pays a monthly income after deduction of interest payments. When the plan-holder dies the loan is repaid out of the proceeds of the house sale.

Home income plans are only for people aged 69 or over. Details of where to find more information on these schemes is listed at the back of the book.

HOUSE INSURANCE

Water-tight: basic standard cover protects houses against disasters such as flooding

For years mortgage lenders have tried to persuade borrowers that buildings and contents insurance are one and the same thing, and that both policies had to be bought from the lender's in-house insurer. This has never been the case and people can make big savings by going elsewhere for cover. **Direct insurers** who forced premiums down in the motor insurance market are now competing heavily on the market for buildings and contents insurance. Mortgage lenders, very worried that they will lose all their custom, are now charging penalties of about £25 if people ask to shop around and buy house insurance elsewhere. Fortunately, many insurers will refund this money for new customers.

Contents insurance

Premiums vary according to the value of the contents, the type and size of home to be insured, and the address. People can opt for basic or standard cover that protects possessions against theft or damage by fire or flood. Comprehensive or all-risk cover is a much wider policy and includes insurance of items taken out of the home. As the name suggests, accidental damage insurance covers possessions damaged in accidents – insurers say most claims come from people who have spilt paint or red wine on furniture or carpets or who have dropped valuable ornaments. Most contents policies are based on a sum assured, the estimated total value of all possessions. It is worth getting this figure right as insurers may scale down payments for people who underinsure and then make claims. Other policies are called 'bedroom rated' and offer a set sum assured according to the number of rooms in the home.

People with high-value possessions can end up paying less for insurance than neighbours of more modest means. Several insurers target rich home owners, and say that they can offer cheap rates because these people tend to have above average security systems and care more for their possessions.

People can qualify for a range of discounts of between 5 and 20 per cent on contents policy premiums. Many insurers give discounts for people with burglar alarms, and with window and door locks. Retired people who tend to be in their homes during the day often pay less, as do people in registered neighbourhood watch areas. The no-claims bonuses common on car insurance policies are also being offered on house contents policies and can reduce the premium cost by up to 25 per cent, and those changing insurers can take previous years' no-claims bonuses with them.

Buildings insurance

This covers a property's structure and pays up if it is destroyed or damaged by explosion, fire or some other disaster. It does not necessarily pay up to repair the effects of subsidence. Mortgage lenders will not offer loans to people without proper buildings insurance, though it is possible to shop around for the best quote. The small print on many policies hides big excesses for different types of claim, the biggest being for subsidence.

The sum assured on a buildings policy refers to a home's rebuilding costs rather than its market value – and these costs have continued to rise throughout the property slump. The Association of British Insurers has a free leaflet explaining how much insurance to buy. People living in non-standard homes – including thatched cottages and converted barns – may have to try specialist insurers and brokers for cover.

I *is for:*

INCOME TAX

It was introduced in 1799 and has been heartily disliked ever since. Governments use it as one of their most successful cash generators and its level has changed over the years according to the country's economic needs and political whims.

It is charged as a percentage of earnings, as the basic thinking behind it was that the more people earned, the more they should pay. At its height in the 1960s, wealthy people paid up to 98 per cent of their income to the Inland Revenue. Today's rates are less penal, and they are often changed in budgets.

Despite plans to simplify the tax system, there are currently three **tax bands**. The first £3,900 of **taxable income** is charged at 20 per cent, any extra income up to £25,500 is charged at 24 per cent and anything above £25,500 is taxed at 40 per cent. It means that someone with £3,900 of taxable income pays £780 a year income tax while someone with £25,500 pays £5,964.

Tax is not paid on every penny earned. Everyone has a **personal allowance**, an amount of money they can receive tax-free each year – the income tax year runs from 6 April one year to 5 April the next. Taxable income is calculated after deducting this allowance from the total income. The basic

Tax shelters allow people to park money away from the taxman's hands

allowance is the single person's allowance of £3,765 a year that applies to everyone, including children. There is both good and bad news for **married couples**. The good news is that they can add an extra £1,790 to their basic allowance; the bad is that the value of a married couple's allowance is limited to 15 per cent of their gross income even if both partners are higher-rate tax payers.

In the past the married couple's allowance was automatically given to husbands and could not be transferred to higher-earning wives. Now couples can elect which partner gets the extra allowance or they can share it between them.

Widows also qualify for a bigger tax allowance for the year in which they are widowed. This is worth £1,790 and is restricted to 15 per cent. Blind people also get the larger allowance.

Older people get extra income tax breaks through **age allowance or relief** – though this is not as simple as it seems. The basic rules are that single people aged 65 to 74 have a personal allowance of £4,910 and this age group also has an increased married couple's allowance of £3,115. Single people aged 75 and over have a personal allowance of £5,090 and the married couple's allowance is £3,155. In both cases the level of the married couple's allowance depends on the age of the older spouse. Confusion arises because age allowance is reduced for people with income of more than £15,200 a year. For each £2 earned over £15,200 a year the age allowance is reduced by £1 until it has gone altogether.

Most employees have income tax deducted automatically from their wages under the Pay-As-You-Earn or **PAYE** system.

Most higher-rate tax payers and a selection of other people are also sent annual **tax returns**. When these have been filled in with details of all the income earned, the Revenue calculates whether more has to be paid or whether the person is in line for a rebate. Bigger bills or rebates can be paid in lump sums as cheques, though smaller ones may be covered through adjustments to annual allowances. In most cases, people asked to complete tax forms will have underpaid tax. As bank and building society interest has 20 per cent deducted from it automatically, higher rate tax payers who complete tax forms and have savings will owe the 20 per cent balance that takes them to the 40 per cent level.

Under the planned move to **self-assessment** of tax, people will be asked to calculate their own liabilities. One element of self-assessment already exists – anyone who is not sent a tax form but who knows they earn extra money that is not taxed is required to request a tax form to declare their extra income. Each year employers should provide **P60** forms that explain how much tax and National Insurance was paid.

The Revenue is the first to admit that mistakes can be made and many people pay too much or too little income tax. Most mistakes creep in on **tax codes**. If these are wrong the amount of tax taken under PAYE may be wrong. Details about tax codes are sent each year with a booklet explaining how they work. Some accountants offer to check tax codes for flat fees of about £25.

The Revenue defines **taxable income** as wages and any other income from sources such as shares, unit or investment trusts or saving accounts. In these circumstances a whole industry of tax avoidance schemes has been set up – all of them are explained in this A–Z guide. The tax shelters – including **Personal Equity Plans, tax-exempt special savings accounts, National Savings** products and **friendly society bonds** – are basically Revenue approved schemes that allow people to keep money out of the taxman's hands and to ensure that any income generated as tax-free is not treated as taxable income. Other tax breaks include Mortgage Interest Relief At Source – or **Miras** – for home buyers, which will be explained under M for Mortgages. Spending on certain items or activities can also be deducted from income before the taxable income figure is calculated.

However, there are **taxable benefits** that can increase income tax bills. The perceived benefit of things such as company cars, free or discount health insurance and so on are factored into tax codes as if they produced actual income. Recipients of the benefits therefore pay extra tax on these benefits.

Local tax offices can offer advice and free leaflets on most tax problems.

INDICES

The London Stock Exchange, in conjunction with the Faculty of Actuaries and the *Financial Times*, has developed a series of indices to cover the UK stock market as well as the main European markets. These indices are calculated to provide a guide to stock market performance.

Some indices such as the **FTSE 100**, or **Footsie** for short, have become household names while others such as the **FTSE**

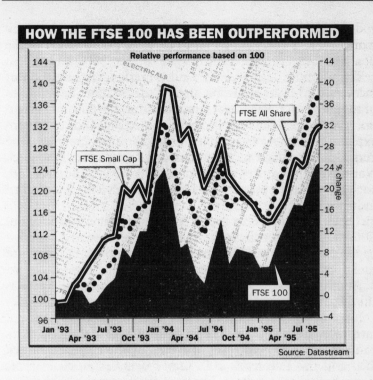

HOW THE FTSE 100 HAS BEEN OUTPERFORMED

Relative performance based on 100

FTSE All Share

FTSE Small Cap

FTSE 100

% change

Jan '93 · Apr '93 · Jul '93 · Oct '93 · Jan '94 · Apr '94 · Jul '94 · Oct '94 · Jan '95 · Apr '95 · Jul '95

Source: Datastream

SmallCap are less well known. The Footsie is an average of the share prices of the biggest 100 companies quoted on the stock market. These companies have a **market capitalisation** of more than £621bn. The larger companies are given more importance by a system of **weighting** to take into account their size. The Footsie is continually updated and is known as a **real time index**. The index began at a **base level** of 1,000 on 3 January 1984 and finished 1995 at 3,689.3.

Since its introduction, the Footsie has spawned a number of **index tracker** unit trusts designed to mirror its performance. Another use for indices such as the Footsie is as a benchmark against which fund managers measure their own performance – all aim to outperform a chosen index to prove their worth.

Other UK indices measure different sections of the stock market. The **FTSE Mid 250** measures the performance of the 250 next biggest companies outside the top 100 and is also a real time index. Companies with a market capitalisation of between £250m and £1.5bn are included. A small number of unit trusts exist which track its performance. The **FTSE 350** index combines the Footsie and the Mid 250 indices to provide a measure of large and medium-sized companies. The companies included account for about 93 per cent of the stock market. Each industry sector within the FTSE Actuaries 350, such as mining or property, also has an index calculated called **industry baskets.**

The **FTSE SmallCap** measures the performance of about 500 of the UK's smallest quoted companies with a market capitalisation between £40m and £250m. This index is not real time but calculated at the end of each day.

Another well-known index, the **FTSE Actuaries All Share**, is the broadest measure of the UK stock market and includes companies above £40m. Footsie has beaten the All Share of late, though the latter is the best performer over the long term.

The European markets are covered by the **FTSE Eurotrack 100** and the **Eurotrack 200**. Other overseas stock markets publish their own indices. The best known are the **Nikkei 225** which covers the Japanese market, the **Dow Jones** which measures United States shares and the **Hang Seng** covering Hong Kong.

INHERITANCE TAX

In the 1994–95 tax year the Inland Revenue grabbed £1.4m in inheritance tax from 18,000 estates – though experts say the tax is relatively easy to avoid.

Anyone who dies with an estate worth less than the tax threshold of £200,000 will not have IHT deducted from their estate. If the total assets left are worth more than £200,000, then IHT is charged at 40 per cent on the excess.

The first way to avoid the tax is to make a **will** or make sure an existing will is up to date. A husband and wife should each have a will so that they can both make use of their own £200,000 exemption. This means a married couple can together leave assets worth £400,000 to their heirs free of IHT without resorting to any complex or costly avoidance schemes.

Another simple way of avoiding IHT is to make use of **gifts**. Any gift made more than seven years before death is exempt from tax. Gifts made within seven years of death will be liable to tax on a sliding scale – the older the gift, the less tax charged. The risk of using the seven-year rule is that it may tempt people to give away too many assets, leaving them without enough money to live on.

People cannot make a gift but then continue to benefit from it, the most common example being to give away a house but continue to live in it. This is called a **gift with reservation** and would be treated as part of an estate for IHT purposes.

Gifts between spouses are exempt from IHT, and people can also make other gifts worth £3,000 per year that are exempt, as are small gifts of less than £250 to any one individual and gifts to charities and national institutions.

A popular but complex way of avoiding IHT is to take out a **life assurance policy** held inside a trust set up to benefit heirs. When a person dies, the proceeds of the policy fall outside the estate for IHT purposes and can be used by the heirs to pay any IHT bill on the rest of the estate.

Investments made in forestry are also free of IHT as are holdings in companies of 25 per cent or more. Investments in unquoted companies such as those listed on the new Alternative Investment Market or included in enterprise investment schemes are taxed at half their value.

People can place assets inside an **accumulation and maintenance trust** and maintain control over them even though they lose technical ownership. The trust protects assets from IHT but can only be used to benefit heirs up to age 25.

A lucky few may be able to use the **official list of exemptions**. This places many valuable articles such as paintings, prints, books, manuscripts and other *objets d'art* outside the Revenue's clutches. Anyone with a valuable object should apply in writing to the Capital Taxes Office in Nottingham. If the object is granted exemption it will be placed on the official list held at the Victoria and Albert Museum in London. One of the conditions of the tax exemption is that the object is available for public display and for museums to borrow. If the object is subsequently sold, IHT becomes payable on the proceeds.

INITIAL CHARGES

These can take the shine off even the best investments. Known as **front-end loads,** they are the commission and expenses that investment or insurance companies deduct from investors' contributions before that money is used to buy shares or investment units. For instance, a 5 per cent initial charge on an investment of £100 means that £5 goes to the investment company, leaving £95 to be put to work on the investor's behalf. The investment then has to grow by £5 just to stand still.

In many cases the initial charge is used to fund commission payments to financial advisers – but they are not reduced if an investor avoids the middleman and goes direct to the investment company. Some initial charges are falling, but others are simply well hidden.

The new rules for **disclosure** were brought in to force companies to reveal what charges they levy on insurance-based funds. **Key features documents** should explain exactly what happens to investors' money. This new regime should soon be applied to unit and investment trusts, so investors can make sure they know what they are paying before they invest.

Initial charges on unit trusts average about 5 per cent, though many new funds are launched with low or no initial charges. In the latter case, investors should check that the investment companies are not making up the difference through bigger annual fees. They should also be wary of relying on the quoted initial charge as the true difference between the price at which investors are sold units and the price they are paid if they cash them in – the **bid/offer spread**. A 5 per cent initial charge suggests that £95 of every £100 is invested. But the bid/offer spread may be worth up to 7 per cent, cutting the initial investment to £93.

Bid/offer spreads are hard to calculate. Investors have to subtract the bid price from the offer price, divide the result by the offer price, and multiply the result by 100. This produces the true bid/offer spread as a percentage.

INSIDER DEALING

The stuff of fictional scandals in films such as *Wall Street* and real crises involving people like American junk-bond king Michael Milken, insider dealing occurs when someone trades in a company's shares after receiving specific information that has not been made public, but which would affect the company's share price if it were widely known.

Anyone from a director to a secretary – and the law has now been toughened to include also any person encouraged to deal after receiving tip-offs from such people – could know a company is about to announce unexpectedly big profits or a major trading deal. If they buy shares before that news is made public, in the hope of making a profit when shares rise, they are guilty of insider dealing. Hasty share sales in advance of bad news are also outlawed.

These shady deals have been illegal since the **Companies Act** of 1980 and the maximum penalty is seven years in prison and/or an unlimited fine. Private investors who buy shares on the basis of anecdotal evidence – knowing workers have been put on overtime, for example – are unlikely to be caught out by insider trading laws.

INVESTMENT CLUBS

The roll call of investment clubs includes groups of real ale drinkers, flight attendants, High Court judges and North Sea oil-rig workers

These have been going strong in America for more than 150 years and are starting to gain converts over here. Investment clubs are groups of friends or workers who decide to pool their assets and expertise to play the stock markets.

There are more than 1,000 such clubs in Britain at the moment – and the list of names shows that members do not have to have any specialised City experience. The roll call of UK clubs includes groups of real-ale drinkers, flight attendants, high court judges and North Sea oil-rig workers. One of the most successful clubs in America is made up of a group of women who met while doing school runs many years ago.

To form an investment club, between three and 20 people have to agree a common investment strategy. They each pay a certain amount of money into the club at set intervals and use the funds to buy a portfolio of shares. Shares are traded whenever the group chooses. Results reveal track records for many investment clubs that put the professionals to shame.

There are certain formalities. The average club has ten members who must all be aged over 18. If more than 20 people apply to join, then the club has to form a limited company and comply with all the requirements of company law such as filing audited accounts. Smaller clubs still have to carry out some official business and must complete forms I85 and I85-2 from the local tax office.

The most efficient clubs have special bank accounts and monthly or quarterly dues are direct debited into the central fund. Some banks have accounts designed specifically for investment clubs and pay interest on cash balances.

Each club should nominate a chairperson, treasurer and secretary, at least two of whom should be required to sign cheques or authorise share trades. These offices can be rotated at regular intervals.

Independent lobby group **ProShare,** which was set up to promote wider share ownership and is a big supporter of investment clubs, states that clubs vary widely. Some take 'steady as they go' approaches and concentrate on big, blue-chip companies, while others go for high-risk speculative dealings. ProShare's staff say that many people take the latter approach as it allows them to spread their risks and to experiment with relatively small amounts of money.

Most investment clubs take an average of £20 a month from members, and the total portfolio and any cash balances are jointly owned in proportion to members' contributions. These clubs usually hold shares through nominee accounts that cut administration and relieve their members of the responsibilities of looking after share certificates. Moreover, the majority have set up **execution-only** arrangements with stockbrokers and call them only when they decide to trade. ProShare points out that only a minority of bigger clubs pay extra for stockbroker's advice, especially as stock selection is all part of the fun of membership.

ProShare has a manual to help people set up and run investment clubs. More details can be found in the useful numbers section.

INVESTMENT TRUSTS

These are companies formed to help private investors find a cheap and easy way into world stock markets. As the charts show, they have done investors proud and outperformed rival unit trusts, deposit accounts and other investment plans.

Investment trusts, which are sometimes called **collective investments**, pool savers' money together, and fund managers invest the total into a portfolio of **shares and bonds**. The idea behind these trusts is to take the difficulty out of investing for ordinary savers who lack the time or skill to make investment decisions themselves.

The first investment trusts were formed in 1868 with the launch of the **Foreign & Colonial Investment Trust**, which is still going strong today. As the name implies, the trust was launched to invest overseas and bought a portfolio of government bonds issued mainly by the new South American republics to finance capital investments in projects such as railways. Such an investment portfolio today, while still possible, would raise a few eyebrows among the mainstream investing public.

Foreign & Colonial now has a very different portfolio and invests for capital growth from UK and overseas shares and is the biggest of the **international general** trusts, the most popular group of trusts among private investors. The biggest trust overall is the £2bn newcomer **3i**, a venture capital trust previously owned by the Bank of England and the main clearing banks.

Investment trusts were immediately popular and there were more than a hundred in existence by the turn of the century. Today there are 338, investing £48bn of savers' assets. The

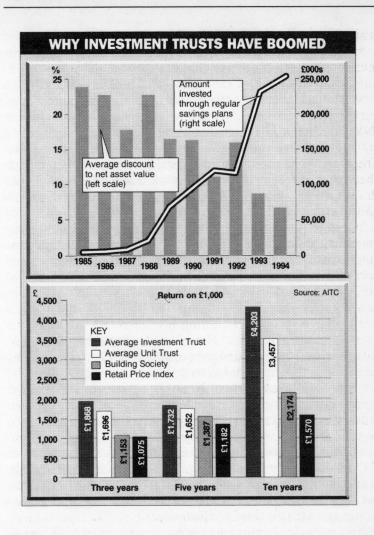

WHY INVESTMENT TRUSTS HAVE BOOMED

Amount invested through regular savings plans (right scale)

Average discount to net asset value (left scale)

Return on £1,000

Source: AITC

KEY
- Average Investment Trust
- Average Unit Trust
- Building Society
- Retail Price Index

Three years: £1,868 / £1,969 / £1,153 / £1,075

Five years: £1,732 / £1,652 / £1,387 / £1,182

Ten years: £4,203 / £3,457 / £2,174 / £1,570

Association of Investment Trust Companies now represents 310 of the main trusts. It provides useful fact sheets and other information, about investment trusts and investment managers as well as performance statistics. Most investment trusts just offer **ordinary shares,** which are quoted on the stock market. **Investment trust share prices** are listed every day in the business sections of national newspapers.

Investors buy shares through a **stockbroker** either when a new trust is launched or afterwards when the shares are traded on the stock market. Over the past ten years the investment trusts themselves have made buying their shares much easier by running investor-friendly **regular saving schemes.** These schemes allow people to invest as little as £20 per month through a direct debit from a bank account. The schemes collect all the monthly investments and then buy a trust's shares en masse. This allows the saving scheme to buy shares at cheap commission rates, thus making them an ideal way for investors to build up capital over the long term. They also impose a useful discipline on savers. Occasional lump sums can also be invested through saving schemes whenever the investor chooses.

Trusts are launched with specific objectives and a huge variety have sprung up offering investors easy access to the world's financial markets. There are now enough trusts to suit all investors. Some are designed to maximise capital growth by investing in the shares of UK companies. Others have the same objective but invest in the shares of companies based overseas in countries such as the United States or Japan. There are also trusts which invest in larger geographical areas such as Europe or the Far East.

Some trusts choose to concentrate on specific industrial sectors such as mining or high technology. Others try to satisfy a specific need such as investing for income. More recently investment trusts have been launched which try to do all these things and are called **split capital trusts.**

Like ordinary companies, investment trusts issue shares to their investors. The investors' money forms the assets of the trust and a board of directors is appointed to look after these assets on behalf of investors. The board normally appoints a trust manager, also known as a fund manager, from a professional investment management company.

The fund manager is allowed to borrow money, either from banks or by issuing bonds to increase assets, in order to take advantage of investment opportunities. This can be risky but aims to give investors higher returns for their money and is known as **gearing**.

As well as borrowing to increase its assets, an investment trust can issue new shares. In the past this has been done through a **rights issue** but this has become unpopular. Trusts now issue **C shares** instead. Investors subscribe to the C share issue and the proceeds are kept separate from the main assets of the trust. They are then invested in an identical portfolio of shares to the main trust and eventually merged with the assets of the trust.

Some trusts add free **warrants** to offers of new ordinary shares as an encouragement to investors. Warrants allow people to buy the shares of a trust for a fixed price at a pre-agreed time in the future. This fixed price is called the **exercise price**. If the ordinary share price rises above the exercise price the warrant holder can make immediate profits by exercising the warrant, acquiring the shares at the lower exercise price and then selling for the higher price quoted on the stock market.

Split capital trusts issue more than just ordinary shares and warrants. To satisfy different investors' needs they issue different **classes** of shares in different combinations. They also have a fixed **wind-up date** when the trust sells all its investments and pays out the proceeds to shareholders.

The classes of shares in a split capital trust are:

- **Zero dividend preference shares** These are low risk investments with predetermined fixed capital returns when trusts wind up. They carry no entitlements to dividends so have no income tax liabilities.
- **Stepped preference shares** These are also low-risk investments offering dividends that rise at a predetermined rate together with fixed redemption values when trusts wind up.

- **Capital shares** These get all assets of a trust when it winds up after other shares have been paid out. Success depends on capital growth outstripping what is required to pay other share classes. They are riskier investments.
- **Income shares** These receive a trust's income. Some have a predetermined repayment value while others have no value when a trust winds up.
- **Highly geared ordinary shares** These offer high income and a share of capital after other classes of shares have been paid out. They combine aspects of income and capital shares.

Investment trusts publish reports and accounts every year like any other company. In the report is published the annual **profit and loss account** and the trust's **balance sheet**. Important figures for investors to look at include a trust's **net asset value (NAV)** which is the total value of assets owned by a trust. This figure can be divided by the number of shares in issue to arrive at a trust's **NAV per share**, which is a measure of each share's value.

But the price of shares on the stock market does not always reflect this value. Sometimes the shares trade below, or at a **discount**, to NAV. Sometimes they will trade above, or at a **premium** to, NAV. This is because a trust's share price is determined by demand and supply from investors. If there is little demand because a trust is out of favour, the share price will slip below its NAV and vice versa. Share price discounts can represent bargains and good money-making opportunities for investors because discounts can narrow and rise towards the NAV figure. This is likely to happen when a trust comes back into favour or becomes the target of a takeover bid.

These days the investment management companies are responsible for most of the new trust launches. They appoint the boards of directors and fund managers. They also appoint stockbrokers to make an offer of shares in a new trust to investors. This has resulted in the investment management companies appointing their own employees to the boards of the investment trusts they manage. Some investors fear this causes a conflict of interest, as the board is supposed to be independent and able to hire and fire investment managers in the interests of the trust's investors. But critics say an investment manager whose employer controls a trust's board is unlikely to get the sack for poor performance.

J is for:

JOBBERS

An extinct species of financial people who were wiped out in one fell swoop by the 1986 **Big Bang**. This was not a mysterious meteorite that happened to hit the City of London but an explosion of new technology coupled with a radical rewriting of the **Stock Exchange** rules that changed the face of the **Square Mile**.

Before 1986 the stock market really was a market, in the sense of buyers and sellers gathered together under one roof to transact business. The floor of the London Stock Exchange on Threadneedle Street across the road from the Bank of England housed numerous pitches equivalent to market stalls. These stalls were each manned by a jobber who would offer shares for sale that he or she owned, which were said to be on his or her book. **Stockbrokers** in search of shares to buy on behalf of their investing clients would approach a jobber having decided which one on the Stock Exchange floor was offering the keenest price. Jobbers also bought shares onto their books from brokers who had clients that wanted to sell, thus supplying a two-way market in shares.

Jobbers made their money by selling shares to brokers at a higher price than they had bought them, known as the jobber's turn. Brokers made their money by charging their clients commission. Before 1986 the Stock Exchange enforced a minimum commission system, which the government eventually decided was a restrictive practice and took the matter to court.

The Stock Exchange agreed to change its ways and inject competition into the cosy, clubby world of stockbroking. Some people look back on the pre-Big Bang days with nostalgia, complaining that today's City of London lacks the sense of community and honour that was prevalent when people met face to face on the Stock Exchange floor. But nostalgia tends to obscure the truth.

Before Big Bang the restrictive practices of the Stock Exchange meant London was out of step and out of date with competing financial centres such as New York. Inefficient stockbrokers were protected by the minimum commission arrangement and customers were losing out as a result. Brokers and jobbers were organised in partnerships and small firms, which meant that the market suffered from a lack of capital. Big institutional investors found it hard to buy substantial amounts of shares because jobbers were often too small to run a sufficiently large book. This lack of **liquidity** was a serious drawback and meant that the stock market was in danger of withering. The good old days were in fact extremely bad.

Abolishing minimum commissions drove the inefficient brokers out of business and forced most of the others into mergers or takeovers by banks, which were now able to add stockbroking to their fast expanding businesses. In fact Big Bang saw the rise of giant, integrated financial firms that combined banking, stockbroking, fund management, foreign exchange and a host of other financial services.

Competition got fierce very quickly and staff were in big demand. This revolution in the City created that 1980s epitome of go-getting selfishness, the **yuppie**. Stripy shirts, red braces, a Porsche or BMW and a fat salary became *de rigueur*. However, competition did have benefits for the consumer in terms of cheaper stockbroking and better products and services.

Instead of splitting the stock-market roles between jobbers and brokers each acting in a single capacity, the Stock Exchange operates a dual capacity system, which means that member firms of the Exchange are called **broker/dealers** and can act for customers as their agent in the role of broker and/or buy and sell shares for themselves in the role of dealer. Firms can also register as a **market maker**, which fulfils the role of the old jobber.

So a stockbroker who receives an order to buy shares has three ways of executing the deal. These are:

1. Buy the required shares from a market maker and charge the client commission – the most common method.
2. Buy the shares from another customer and sell them on to the original customer, charging both parties commission.
3. Sell the customer shares that the stockbroker already owns.

Buying from a market maker, who can only deal with Stock Exchange member firms, involves a broker ringing up the market maker and agreeing the deal over the telephone. The old Stock Exchange floor is no longer used. Brokers can see the price of shares on a screen in their office called the **Stock Exchange Automated Quotation System** or SEAQ. Market makers quote prices for more than 2,000 shares on SEAQ which is normally on the same screen in a broker's office as the **TOPIC** system, which is a market and company news system. As well as the buy-and-sell price for a share, market makers also quote the minimum number of shares normally traded, which is called the **normal market size**. A glance at the SEAQ entry for any particular share will tell a broker what the best buy and sell prices are, known as the **touch price**, and which market makers are offering those prices. This way of organising a stock market is called a quote-driven market.

SEAQ is not an automated trading system, it is purely a noticeboard for displaying share prices and other information about a share. There is an automated dealing facility provided by the Stock Exchange called **SAEF** (SEAQ Automated Execution Facility), although this is only for small deals. New changes to the way the stock market is organised are likely to be introduced, including an order-driven market which matches buyers and sellers.

JOINT INVESTMENTS

Many couples choose to share ownership of everything from houses to bank accounts. There are two basic ways of sharing assets, holding them as **joint owners** or as **tenants in common**. Both systems apply to unmarried as well as married couples.

Savings accounts and other investments tend to be held under the *joint ownership* rules. Houses can also be held this way. The arrangement means that the assets are shared equally between both partners regardless of who actually pays for them. If one partner dies, their share of the asset passes directly to the surviving partner.

People can also choose to hold assets as *tenants in common*. This allows people to split ownership in other ratios rather than just splitting it equally. This proportion can more accurately reflect who pays, say, the mortgage. When a house or other asset is held by tenants in common, one person can leave his or her share to anyone in a will. Problems arise if someone in this situation dies without a will as the house will be passed on according to the laws of intestacy, so the other partner may not necessarily inherit it.

Many people base the decision on ownership on the **inheritance tax** implications of each arrangement. Bills can be cut by having a property held as tenants in common with each partner deciding to pass their share to their children on death – as long as the children are guaranteed not to force the survivor out of the house in their lifetime. When the second partner dies the total estate is reduced as half the house value has already been given away, reducing the total tax bill.

It is useful to have some savings accounts held jointly. If a couple's assets are in the name of the partner who dies, the survivor may have to wait until probate has been granted before being able to withdraw any money. Holding accounts jointly means the survivor has normal access to funds. Unless stated otherwise, most joint savings accounts are deemed to come under the rules of joint ownership rather than those of tenants in common.

JOINT-LIFE ASSURANCE

Two people – normally married couples – can take out joint-life assurance contracts to pay out on the death of either the first or second named person on the policy. The policies can be **term assurance** or **whole-of-life assurance**. Term assurance pays out on deaths that occur within a specific period, such as ten years. Whole-of-life policies pay out whenever death occurs.

A husband and wife can take out a joint term assurance policy and choose to have it pay out on the first death. This means that the surviving spouse, be it husband or wife, will receive a cash lump sum on the death of the other partner.

Joint-life assurance that pays out on the second death can be useful for tax planning purposes. On the death of a husband an estate normally passes to the wife through the husband's will and no inheritance tax is payable. But on the death of the wife, the estate is likely to pass to any children and inheritance tax may well be payable this time around. But the cash proceeds of a life assurance policy written to pay out on the second death (the wife's in this example) can be used by the children to pay off any inheritance tax bill. The policy must be held in trust, outside the estate, for this to work.

Joint-life assurance can be more expensive than a single life policy because insurers are faced with double the chance of a payout. Also, a husband and wife may be better off taking out two single life policies to produce two separate payments, and in many cases advisers recommend that couples take out separate life policies to vary the amount of cover between partners.

JUNK BONDS

Junk bonds are issued by growing companies that want to raise capital to expand their existing business or mount takeovers

These bonds are an infamous form of investment that came to prominence in the United States during the early 1980s. They featured in various Wall Street scandals towards the end of the decade and forced their prime advocate, investment firm **Drexel Burnham Lambert**, to seek protection from its creditors under Chapter 11 of the US bankruptcy laws.

Like normal bonds, junk bonds are issued by growing companies that want to raise capital to expand their existing business or mount takeovers. The big difference is the level of **income** or **yield** paid by the bonds. Junk bonds are issued with a much higher yield than usual to compensate investors for their higher risks.

Large companies pay for **credit ratings** from agencies such as **Standard & Poor's** or **Moodys**. These ratings reflect the financial strength of companies issuing bonds. The most credit worthy and thus least risky companies are given a **triple A rating** and can pay the lowest interest on their bonds. The small or less well-known companies that issue junk bonds have no credit rating and must pay a higher rate of interest to attract investors as a result.

Junk bonds are issued almost exclusively in the United States by US companies. There have been no recognised junk bond issues in the UK, but City experts believe this may change over the next two or three years. The Chancellor of the Exchequer is keen to encourage companies to issue bonds and recently introduced **Corporate Bond Personal Equity Plans** to boost demand for them. It is expected this initiative will lead to high-yield bonds being issued in Britain.

Junk bonds have proved successful for both issuing companies and investors in the United States despite their tarnished image. The issuing of such bonds gives small companies access to big institutions with capital to invest and is said to encourage entrepreneurs.

The bonds have proved a good investment too. Between 1984 and 1994, for every $100 invested in junk bonds, only $1.60 was lost through bankruptcy. At the same time, junk bonds were paying 2.6 per cent over the average yield for top-rated bonds, giving a net gain in yield of 1 per cent for taking the extra risk.

They are also becoming more popular. Companies are raising money through junk bonds to reorganise their finances. Capital raised from junk bonds can be used to pay off bank debts. Bonds can be repaid at a much later date than bank loans, which gives companies more time to be successful. Although the interest rate demanded by bond investors is higher than on bank loans, companies are still better off. Thus new junk bond issues in 1990 were $1bn, peaked in 1993 at $53bn and in 1995 were a healthy $30bn.

Sometimes the term 'junk bond' is used to describe the

bonds of companies which have fallen on hard times and run into difficulties. If this happens, the chances of the issuing company missing an interest payment or going bust are much greater. The price of the bonds falls and yield rises. But true junk bonds are those specifically issued with a high yield.

K is for:

KRUGERRANDS

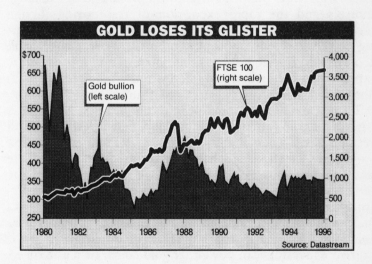

GOLD LOSES ITS GLISTER

Gold bullion (left scale)

FTSE 100 (right scale)

Source: Datastream

These are gold coins minted in South Africa and used by investors as a convenient way of holding physical gold. But there are several other ways to invest in gold.

Gold has always been seen as a store of value. The traditional wisdom held that by putting wealth into gold, investors were protecting themselves against the ravages of inflation or a depreciating currency. Its universal appeal also made it an attractive investment in time of financial and political upheaval.

But sadly, gold has not bestowed the Midas touch on investors. As the chart on page 115 shows, the metal has traded in a narrow price range for the past decade although early 1996 showed signs of a rally. Investors are deserting it as a means of protecting assets against inflation or currency devaluation or uncertainty in the markets. The 1987 global stock-market crash, the Gulf War and the collapse of the European Exchange Rate Mechanism are all major upheavals that have had little impact on the price of gold.

These days it is easier and more profitable to inflation-proof assets with other financial instruments. The end of exchange controls and the rapid expansion of fast-moving foreign exchange markets means people can switch out of depreciating currencies easily and quickly. Furthermore, unlike bank deposits and bonds, gold pays no interest, and it is therefore expensive to hold when real interest rates (adjusted for inflation) are high. It is also expensive to insure.

Yet despite all this, some people cannot resist gold's lure. Figures for gold demand show that Japanese investors are still keen on it. Gold demand hit a record 1,793 tonnes in the first six months of 1995, much of it accounted for by Japanese investors hoarding gold bars after the uncertainties of the Kobe earthquake and the gas attacks on the Tokyo underground system. Other big holders of gold are central banks such as the Bank of England, and Far Eastern investors who hold large amounts of gold in the form of jewellery.

Private investors can buy either gold coins, such as Krugerrands or sovereigns, or gold bars from retail dealers in London such as Gold Investments and the Bolivian & General Tin Trust. Gold bars come in sizes that start at 5 grams and rise through 10, 20, 50 and 100 grams up to the 1 kg bar. There is also a 1 oz bar. Gold bars should be stamped with the name of a reputable carrier such as Johnson Mathey in the UK or

Credit Suisse or UBS in Switzerland. The stamp means the bar is of the correct weight and content.

A single Krugerrand which contains one ounce of gold costs about £253; a sovereign which contains half that much gold costs about £63. The cost of gold coins has fallen recently, thanks to a directive on value added tax from the European Union which states that second-hand coins are exempt from the tax. VAT at 17.5 per cent is payable only on the dealer's commission.

Investments in gold need not necessarily involve a physical holding in the metal – indeed it can be more expensive to hold it, as buyers who have gold delivered to them in the UK have to pay value added tax on the purchase price. This can be avoided by holding gold offshore – though storage costs have to be put into the equation. The **World Gold Council** can advise on how to buy gold and who to buy it from.

Some investors prefer to buy the shares of companies that mine gold or are involved in the gold-producing process in some other way. Investors can also put money into **unit or investment trusts** that are designed to invest in a wide portfolio of gold-related shares. The most successful of these is the Mercury Gold and General unit trust run by Julian Baring at Mercury Asset Management. It has produced a 26 per cent annual compound return over the past five years – a much better performance than the gold price itself.

The gold price is fixed twice daily by five leading City firms that regularly trade the metal.

L is for:

LIBOR

This stands for the London interbank offered rate and is important to the banks in their dealings with each other and with the big institutions that issue bonds either for themselves or their corporate clients. But in recent years Libor has been thrust upon consumers in the mortgage market. Some lenders have been offering loans with an interest rate linked to Libor.

As the name suggests Libor is the rate at which banks will lend money to each other. This gives it an important role as a benchmark for other interest rates, such as the rates paid on a bond. Often a bond will be issued with a rate quoted as being so many basis points over Libor. There are 100 basis points in 1 per cent, so a bond that pays interest at 50 basis points over Libor will be paying 0.5 per cent more than Libor. With Libor-linked mortgages borrowers typically pay between 1 and 1.5 per cent over Libor (100–150 basis points).

Libor-linked mortgages came to prominence in the 1980s but have since proved unable to beat the very aggressive competition in the form of discount and fixed-rate loans now being marketed by lenders. Libor is set every quarter so the interest rate on Libor-linked mortgages can change every quarter. This is an advance if interest rates are falling, as the benefit of this will be passed on more quickly than with a standard mortgage. If rates are rising this is obviously a drawback.

LIFE ASSURANCE

This is the essential element on any wealth check – but it is all too often overlooked. Surveys show most people have too little life cover to protect their families after their deaths, even though cover can be cheaper than expected.

Life assurance is something of a misnomer. The event that the policies offer protection against is not life but death. The proceeds of a policy go to help surviving loved ones over the trauma of death by providing financial assistance. Death insurance would probably be a more accurate title for the policies but no right-minded insurer would want to market a policy called death. Despite its somewhat morbid overtones life assurance is very important. The protection it offers is likely to prove vital to those dependants you leave behind, either to meet your outstanding debts or to provide them with much needed cash at times of distress.

Life assurance is most commonly sold when someone takes out a mortgage. The lender will insist on the cover to make sure that a loan will be repaid in the event of a borrower's death. However, people really should think about extending life assurance cover beyond the amount of any outstanding loan, to make sure, for instance, that adequate funds are available for several years should a parent die. It is not just the bread winner who should be insured. At the risk of using outdated sexual stereotypes, it is still possible these days that a mother may be undertaking most of the domestic duties of a household, probably bringing up young children, and earning far less than her partner able to work full time. This does not mean that her life should not be adequately insured. If she should die, the cost of her partner replacing her in her domes-tic duties with hired help, or indeed giving up full-time work to carry on her role, can be extremely heavy. So anyone with

Clients are asked to take a medical when applying for more than a set amount of cover

dependants and/or expensive responsibilities to others needs to be properly covered.

There are two basic types of cover: **term assurance** and **whole-of-life assurance**. As the name suggests, *term policies* last for a set number of years, often 25 years to cover the length of a mortgage. Holders pick the amount of cover they want, the **sum assured,** and if they die within the term their estates will be paid the sum assured. If they survive to the end of the term, then the policy lapses. These are the cheapest life policies because there is no investment element and the policyholder will not be paid anything if they want to cash plans in early.

Premiums have been falling recently and, in many cases, people who took out term policies five years ago could discontinue them and start new ones for lower premiums. One reason for this was the Aids scare of the middle and late 1980s. The people who price term assurance, known as **underwriters,** feared that the HIV virus would spread very quickly among both homosexual and heterosexual groups. Anyone applying for term assurance at this time who showed even the smallest likelihood of being involved with what insurers considered 'high risk' groups or activities were charged high premiums. Since the Aids epidemic has failed to materialise in this country the re-rating of life assurance policies of the 1980s has been undone and premiums for the cover are increasingly attractive.

Unlike term assurance, *whole-of-life policies* do not have set terms and pay out whenever the policyholder dies. They also carry **surrender values** and **paid-up values** so that people can get something back if they are forced to stop paying premiums after a few years.

Most whole-of-life policies charge set premiums throughout their lives, though, in common with term policies, the original premiums vary according to holders' ages when policies are taken out. They can also vary according to the policyholder's occupation, and people with pre-existing medical conditions may be refused cover or have premiums increased or **loaded** to match the greater risk of claims. Insurers normally ask people to have medicals if they are applying for more than a set amount of cover. It is a mistake to lie on medical or other application forms as insurers can refuse to pay out on policies if they discover an existing risk was not disclosed on application. Some insurers now offer new **lifestyle discounts** for non-smokers or for people who conform to set weight, fitness and other criteria.

Life policies carry a range of options to make them stand out from a crowd.

For example:

- People can buy **convertible term policies** that can be turned into whole-of-life policies after a few years if the holder can afford the higher premiums.
- **Renewable** policies offer guaranteed acceptance for new policies when original term policies expire, regardless of the holder's new age or state of health. Premiums for these policies are more expensive than standard policies.
- People can also buy policies with increasing, decreasing or index-linked sums assured. Decreasing sum-assured policies are suitable for people with repayment mortgages where the capital sum that needs to be covered falls each year.
- **Joint-life** policies also exist, and couples can choose to have benefits paid on either the first or second death.
- **Endowment** policies, which combine insurance and investment plans, are explained in detail under the letter M for Mortgage.

Many people are given 'free' life cover through personal or company pension plans and may have small amounts of cover in other investment schemes such as friendly society policies and maximum investment plans. This should be taken into account when working out how much life cover is required for a new mortgage. Experts say people with families should have cover worth the equivalent of ten years' wages. Single people without dependants have less need for life cover and should consider term policies if at all.

The Association of British Insurers has a series of leaflets on life cover. The address to write to is listed at the back of the book.

LLOYD'S OF LONDON

Lloyd's used to epitomise quality and fair play in the City of London but now has an image tainted by corruption scandals and big losses. It has succeeded in forcing many previously well-off people into penury. The less sympathetic observers say there has been one positive outcome of the Lloyd's debacle – the dramatic increase in the number of bed-and-breakfast businesses springing up across the British countryside in some of the country's more desirable homes as beleaguered Lloyd's investors try to make a living. Such caustic remarks are typical of the strength of feeling that Lloyd's generates in people. For many, the well-heeled, middle-class individuals whose capital provided the backing for Lloyd's complex insurance operation have only themselves to blame for being too greedy and too complacent to check exactly what they were getting into. But the people who have been ruined by Lloyd's losses say that in many instances they were the victims of one of the biggest corruption scandals this country has ever seen.

Lloyd's is a market. Just as the stock market is the market for companies' shares, Lloyd's is a market for insurance policies. It is not the only insurance market. People can go to insurance companies for policies or try other rival insurance markets such as the **Institute of London Underwriters**. But Lloyd's sets itself apart from other insurance markets in the way it is organised and the range of risks people can find insurance for under one roof. Lloyd's supplies cover to protect individuals and companies against a vast range of risks. Policies pay out if ships sink or footballers break their legs as well as more mundane events such as car thefts and burglaries.

The market began in the 1680s in a coffee house near London's Tower Wharf where ship owners and sea captains regularly met to discuss maritime issues. Merchants agreed to insure ships and their cargoes in return for a down payment or **premium**, and ship insurance remained the backbone of the new market when it moved to larger premises above London's Royal Exchange.

The trappings of its seventeenth-century origins are still retained by Lloyd's. Anyone visiting its headquarters will see frock-coated staff walking around the Lutine Bell on the main underwriting floor. The bell, from a captured French frigate, was rung to signal news of overdue ships – once for bad news, twice for good. These traditional paraphernalia are now housed in the Lloyd's Building at No. 1 Lime Street. Ironically, the move to this hi-tech home coincided with a downturn in the market's fortunes.

In the late 1980s it was rocked by scandal as various high-profile Lloyd's **underwriters** and **brokers** ended up in court, charged with defrauding the market. Since then a series of disasters such as the Piper Alpha oil rig explosion, hurricanes Betsy and Hugo, and the rise of asbestos-linked claims from the United States have pushed the insurance market into debt.

This debt has hit **Lloyd's Names** worst of all. Sometimes called **members**, Names are the rich individuals whose personal wealth supports the market. Lloyd's agrees to insure a risk because it knows that the Names have agreed to pay all justifiable claims. Names are said to have **unlimited liability** as a result. Names must provide proof that they have £250,000 of unencumbered assets, excluding their main house, before they can join. Some Names take on more business than others and are called **high liquidity Names** who must show £500,000 of wealth.

Membership of Lloyd's has to be proposed by two existing Lloyd's professionals and involves paying a deposit of between 25 to 30 per cent of the premiums accepted. They then attend the Rota Committee where the chairman asks if the potential Name understands that under the unlimited liability rules they are liable to pay for claims down to their last penny. In recent years many have had this brought home to them in no uncertain terms.

There are now 14,800 Names compared to 31,000 at the market's peak in 1988–89. About one if five of Lloyd's Names work as underwriters and brokers and are known as **working**

Names. They have been accused by non-working Names, faced with huge bills, of keeping the best risks to themselves.

Although Names are liable for losses as individuals, they group together in **syndicates** when it comes to accepting business. A Name can join more than one syndicate to reduce risks. A syndicate is represented in the Lloyd's market by an **underwriter** who accepts risks on its behalf. The administrative affairs of a syndicate are looked after by a **managing agent.** The affairs of individual Names are looked after by a **member's agent** who also normally acts as a sponsor for a prospective Name.

After all its recent problems Lloyd's has recently allowed companies with at least £1.5m to spare to become **corporate members** with the added advantage of limited liability. Dozens of investment trusts called **Lloyd's trusts** have been formed to poll investors' assets to take advantage of the limited liability rule change.

Lloyd's works on a three-year accounting period because of the amount of time claims take to come to light and be paid. Claims outstanding for longer are called **long-tail business.** After five years of losses, which peaked at £2.5bn in 1990, analysts predict profits of £1bn for 1993. Lloyd's investment trusts are expected to pay bigger dividends when past losses have fallen out of the equation.

The trouble with Lloyd's is that it is on the verge of collapse unless an ambitious rescue plan – far from certain to succeed – is initiated. Lloyds has made losses totalling more than £8bn in five years. Thousands of Lloyd's Names have refused to pay their claims bills, citing either bankruptcy or negligence on the part of Lloyd's in accepting certain costly risks in the first place. The hope is that a planned new insurance company, which Lloyd's has formed with the help of several top financial experts in the City of London and called **Equitas,** will take on responsibility for past losses such as those arising from US asbestos-linked claims. By taking on these liabilities Equitas will allow Lloyd's to draw a line under the losses of the late 1980s and early 1990s and provide breathing space for a 'new

Lloyd's' to emerge. But Equitas needs capital to work. Names are being asked to pay into Equitas, as are various other groups involved in Lloyd's, as a final settlement of their debts and an exit route from unlimited liability. They will then be free once and for all of Lloyd's. But the likely total cost of Equitas has raised concerns. An end to the Lloyd's nightmare is in sight for Names, but it could prove an expensive solution.

LONG-TERM CARE INSURANCE

This is a new type of cover designed to pay for the cost of **residential and nursing homes** for the elderly – a crucial subject as the population ages and state benefits fall.

Nearly 30 per cent of elderly people are in nursing and residential homes and this figure is expected to rise in line with life expectancy figures. The big problem is the cost of this care. About 72 per cent of people in long-term care or nursing homes cannot meet the £300 to £400 costs per week, and so turn to means-tested benefits to make up the difference.

The situation is becoming increasingly difficult. Long-term care can cost anything between £12,000 and £17,000 per year, and charges are rising faster than inflation. Anyone with assets, including their home, of £16,000 or more in savings, will not qualify for state help. Many people are forced to sell their homes and other possessions to pay for care bills – making a mockery of John Major's dreams of a society in which wealth cascades down the generations.

Politicians are wrestling with how they can help people with these costs and protect their assets such as homes from being sold off. It is becoming a big political issue for all parties in the House of Commons. How private insurance can combine with the government's policies for the welfare state is being hotly debated and discussed by politicians and insurance chiefs. Both Labour and Conservative politicians, while remaining committed to some notion of welfare benefits for those who need them, believe that people need to be encouraged to do more to help themselves and protect their standards of living through private insurance.

Long-term care insurance is just one type of private insurance that could provide this sort of extra protection, alongside better pension provision either through company pensions or personal pensions, to make people's old age more comfortable. Others believe that a **social insurance fund** is required into which people are forced to pay today to cover their costs tomorrow.

Another idea is to encourage people to buy long-term care insurance through **incentives** or **tax breaks**. There are two types of suitable insurance: **pre-funded** or **immediate need policies**. *Pre-funded policies* charge monthly or lump-sum premiums and promise to pay incomes to meet care costs. Premiums depend on a customer's age – at the moment they are mainly bought by people in their late fifties or sixties. A 55-year-old man would pay £41.38 per month or a lump sum of £8,067 for an income of £1,000 per month. One problem with these policies is that funds cannot be reclaimed even if the policy is never used. *Immediate need plans* provide income from endowments that mature monthly. The worse a policyholder's health is when starting a plan, the lower the premiums.

So far few people have been persuaded to take out long-term care insurance policies, though insurers are stepping up their sales drives. The Association of British Insurers has laid down a code of practice for salesmen to follow and there are calls to include long-term care policies within the Financial Services Act to add an extra layer of protection to customers.

$\mathcal{M}$ is for:

MEDICAL INSURANCE

Private medical insurance offers people an alternative to **National Health Service care.** PMI policies are available from a growing number of insurers and are fast becoming an important topic for politicians as the NHS struggles to cope under ever-increasing demand for its services.

The question of whether people should be given tax breaks or incentives to take out PMI as a replacement for relying on the NHS will be a central question for both Labour and the Conservatives at the next general election. At the moment, people over 60 receive **tax relief** on the premiums they pay for PMI. It is possible these concessions could be extended to encourage more people to take out policies, thus relieving the burden on the NHS, but the Labour Party has said it intends to stop this tax break rather than extend it to others. Other proposals include a plan to allow people to pay the NHS for higher levels of care over and above the basic level available to all.

The big players in the medical insurance market are **Bupa, Western Provident Association (WPA), Norwich Union Healthcare** and **Private Patient's Plan (PPP),** although there are numerous other smaller players in the market. At the moment PMI remains a matter of personal choice and people who take out policies still have to pay the normal amount of income tax to fund the NHS. However, demand for private cover is growing fast. By the end of 1994 there were 6.6 million people covered – a 4 per cent increase on 1993. On current trends this number will reach 9m by the year 2000 – equivalent to one person in six.

One of the reasons why people take out policies is to spread the cost of private medical care. Outpatient consultations can cost between £30 and £90 in the private sector. A varicose vein operation can cost between £1,000 and £1,500 and a hernia operation between £1,200 and £2,000, depending on where patients live and what kind of hospital they go to. Prices rise for more complicated operations. A private hospital would charge between £7,000 and £15,000 for a heart bypass operation and between £5,000 to £20,000 for cancer treatment.

Latest figures show that a couple in the West Midlands (male aged 66, female aged 67) would pay between £83 and £183 a month for comprehensive medical insurance cover. A young family in Sussex (father 36, mother 32, children six and four) would pay between £60 and £109 a month for comprehensive cover. Certainly cost is an important issue when buying medical insurance, but it should not be the only consideration. A good tip is to work out exactly what benefits are being offered from a selection of policies and then decide which one offers the best value for money. Experts say people should still see the NHS as the place to go for emergencies, but private hospitals paid for by insurance policies are convenient and reliable when it comes to treating less immediate problems.

The best way to obtain medical insurance is to join an **employer's company-paid scheme**, if there is one. These are offered by many companies as staff perks. If, however, people have to pay for their own cover they have a choice of two broad types of policy: **comprehensive** or **budget**. Unfortunately, higher premiums do not always mean better cover, so customers should read the small print before joining up.

- Most policies offer different **bands** of cover such as A, B or C. The higher the band, the more luxurious the hospital, but the level of medical treatment will be the same, regardless of accommodation scale.
- Potential policyholders should also ask if a policy offers a full refund of medical costs or only a proportion. In the latter case, policyholders either have to join an NHS waiting list for further treatment or pay for any shortfalls themselves.
- Budget cover will limit the hospital that policyholders can choose and may also omit outpatient costs, which can be high.
- Some schemes will only pay for treatment if policyholders cannot receive NHS treatment within **six weeks**.

Buyers should also ask how insurers assess risk. Some policies are fully underwritten. With these policies insurers ask consumers for their medical history and then advise them of any restrictions to their cover. They assess people on their own merits and may ignore past conditions if the risk of a repeat is small. Other policies will cover anyone without the need for medical evidence, but automatically exclude conditions suffered in the past five years. These insurers will only cover conditions that arise after the policies are taken out. Such policies are said to have a **moratorium** on existing conditions.

These are important points to remember if people switch insurers to save money or leave a company scheme when moving jobs. Switching from one medical insurance policy to another should not be done without careful thought and a close examination of the terms and conditions of both policies.

Policyholders can reduce premiums by agreeing to pay a proportion of medical bills themselves, as well as claiming tax relief if they are over 60. Some policies will also offer **no-claims discounts**, as with car insurance, and **loyalty bonuses** that limit the normal, age-related premium increases occurring every five or ten years.

People should avoid schemes that will not provide cover for

those above a certain age – these mean that people will be forced to leave schemes just when they are likely to need them most. Other schemes will have a maximum entry age but will cover people for life once they have joined.

For self-employed people the cheapest way to buy medical insurance is often to form a **small company scheme** for a few people – the big insurers can say how these work. One final option for many people is **self-insurance**. This involves saving or investing money specifically to cover the cost of any future treatments as and when they arise – the crucial thing is to continue to pay into this personal fund and not to dip into it for other purposes.

Medical insurance is currently treated as **general insurance**. As a result the marketing and sale of PMI does not fall within the terms of the Financial Services Act. There is a voluntary code of sales practice published by the **Association of British Insurers** but medical insurance sales organisations do not have to join. Tales of malpractice and mis-selling have prompted the **Office of Fair Trading (OFT)** to investigate the business over fears that lack of information means consumers are not getting value for money. The OFT intends to examine whether medical insurance policies have unfair or obscure exclusions. It will also look at whether consumers receive the kind of payouts they expected. The industry is still waiting for its findings.

MORTGAGES

Borrowing money to buy a home remains the biggest financial commitment most people will undertake. Five years of falling property prices has not cooled the nation's obsession with owner occupation and the housing market is still a central driving force behind consumer confidence and spending in the economy.

A mortgage is money lent by a bank, building society or insurance company to a person who wants to buy a home. The

MONTHLY COST OF £60,000 MORTGAGE

REPAYMENT	4% RATE	10% RATE
Payment to lender	£306.70	£514.44
Decreasing term assurance	£7.80	£7.80
Total	**£314.50**	**£522.24**

ENDOWMENT	4% RATE	10% RATE
Payment to lender	£185.00	£462.50
Endowment premium	£88.96	£88.96
Total	**£273.96**	**£551.46**

PEP	4% RATE	10% RATE
Payment to lender	£185.00	£462.50
PEP premium	£76.63	£76.63
Level term assurance	£10.06	£10.06
Total	**£271.69**	**£549.19**

Source: London & Country Mortgages
The insurance is based on a male aged 30 borrowing £60,000
The mortgage is taken over 25 years, with 15% MIRAS

lender expects the loan, including interest, to be repaid over a set number of years but gives the borrower a choice of how to make the repayment.

To encourage people to buy their own homes the government grants **mortgage interest tax relief (Miras)** at the rate of 15 per cent on the first £30,000 of any home loan. This has been whittled down over the years as consecutive chancellors have sought easy tax cuts. This is no bad thing according to many economists who fear tax incentives to buy bricks and mortar distort overall spending patterns.

In the past most mortgages were granted by building societies. They provided loans mainly linked to an insurance policy called an **endowment** which was designed to repay both interest and capital. After an Act of Parliament in 1986 building societies were allowed to be far more flexible in their lending habits and the home loans market has become increasingly competitive. New lenders have come into the market and challenged the dominance of the building societies and high-street banks.

About 60 per cent of people who apply for a home loan still end up with an endowment mortgage. The schemes work by a borrower making monthly payments into a policy either supplied by the lender or an insurance company tied to the lender. The regular payments are then split. One portion goes to paying off the interest. The other portion is destined to pay off the capital and is placed in a **with-profits** or unit-linked insurance fund, which in turn invests in a mixture of shares, bonds and property. The borrower hopes this investment will grow sufficiently to repay the loan capital and leave some over as a cash lump sum for people to spend as they wish.

The endowment policy also includes **life assurance**, which pays out a sum big enough to repay the mortgage if the borrower dies. Life assurance is required with all types of mortgage.

The big advantage of an endowment mortgage is its convenience: it is a ready-made mortgage package which takes care of interest repayments, and investment to repay capital and life assurance. But to get the benefits of an endowment a borrower needs to hold on to it until **maturity**. This is when the proceeds are paid out including bonuses which are awarded each year the policy is in force plus a final one-off bonus called a **terminal** bonus. If endowments are cashed in before their maturity date borrowers will receive a poor return in the form of a **surrender value**, which in the early years of a policy may be less than they have paid in.

This rigid structure has resulted in endowments being heavily criticised by organisations such as the **Office of Fair**

Trading for being poor value for money, inflexible and often sold to unsuited customers. Some short-term ten-year endowments sold before the 1987 stock-market crash have raised concerns that they would fall short of their repayment targets, forcing customers to increase their monthly payments.

Nevertheless, despite the criticism not all endowments are bad for borrowers planning for the long term. Good ones are a low-risk way of repaying a mortgage. Once someone has bought an endowment they should be able to keep it going and use it to repay future mortgages from different lenders when they move house. Monthly endowment payments can also be topped up to cover a bigger loan.

There have also been improvements in the way endowments are sold. Borrowers must now be told in pounds and pence how much the policies cost and how much of their premiums are being eaten up in charges.

Other mortgage schemes are becoming more popular. One is the simple **repayment mortgage** preferred by about 30 per cent of borrowers. A lender adds up how much interest is payable over the period of a loan, often 25 years, plus the capital sum. Monthly repayments are then calculated to pay off interest and capital at the same time. This means that the outstanding debt is reduced bit by bit over the term of the loan and allows borrowers to build up **equity** in the property without relying on rising house prices. Because there is no investment growth assumed in a repayment mortgage the monthly repayments may be higher than an endowment, especially in the early years or at lower interest rates, but they do not expose borrowers to stock market risks.

For people who move regularly repayment mortgages have their drawbacks. In the early years repayments mainly meet interest rather than capital, so borrowers who move every few years will never eat into the amount they owe. But they do have advantages. By building up equity in a home borrowers can move more easily and avoid one of the most insidious features of the 1990s property market – **negative equity**.

Falling house prices since 1989 mean about 1.1 million

Escaping negative equity is hard. One way is to sit tight and pray for a sudden surge in house prices

borrowers (10 per cent of mortgaged homes) own properties that are worth less than their outstanding mortgages. The spectre of negative equity is more prevalent in the south of England than anywhere else and generally affects first-time buyers who bought between 1988 and 1991. The average amount of negative equity is £7,000 but can rise to £9,500 in Greater London and the south-east compared to £3,000 in the north-west. Areas such as Northern Ireland, which is enjoying a mini house price boom, and Scotland are free of the problem. The national amount of negative equity is £7bn.

Escaping negative equity is hard. One way is to sit tight and pray for a sudden surge in house prices. Experts say a 5 per cent rise in house prices would free half the negative equity sufferers and five years of 5 per cent rises would cure the nation as a whole. Another simple solution is to use savings to meet any unpaid mortgage debt when selling. For those not moving immediately but reticent about relying on house prices to eradicate negative equity, putting money aside over a few years is a good idea. But for those who can sell their house and need to move, the answer is more complicated. The easiest solution is to decant the negative equity into a new 100 per cent mortgage when moving. Thus someone with a £70,000 mortgage on a house worth just £63,000 who wants to move to a house worth £80,000 can do so by carrying the £7,000 of negative equity forward through a new mortgage of £87,000. This reschedules the debt but does not wipe it out. Only the most creditworthy borrowers with spotless repayment records will be allowed to make use of such schemes.

Negative equity coupled with the effects of the last recession have proved too much for some borrowers, who have been forced out of properties they can no longer afford. In these cases lenders have had to **repossess**. They then sell the property to try and minimise their losses. Any shortfall is met by a **mortgage indemnity** insurer.

This insurance benefits the lender but is paid for by the borrower and premiums can be several hundred pounds. If a bank or building society has to make a claim on its indemnity policy, the insurer will pay up and then pursue the borrower for the money. Borrowers with a large deposit will pay much lower indemnity premiums and with a 25 per cent deposit will normally escape the insurance altogether. A repayment mortgage helps borrowers build up equity which can be used as a deposit for a new property, reducing the size of the insurance premium.

Since the mid-1980s the mortgage market has become more flexible. These days there are a number of alternatives to the endowment or the repayment mortgage. Some borrowers prefer to link their home loan with their **pension**. This allows people to make contributions to a personal pension plan on which they receive back any income tax. On retirement a portion of the pension fund pays off the mortgage although most people expect long-term price rises to have outstripped the size of the outstanding debt, thus leaving them free of mortgage commitments when they move house.

Banks and building societies are making greater use of **interest-only mortgages**. These mean a lender makes a loan and expects borrowers just to pay off the interest. It takes no responsibility for how borrowers repay the capital sum out-standing after the term of the mortgage, be it ten, 20, or 25 years. How this lump sum is repaid lies entirely with the borrower. This makes mortgages more flexible but also poten-tially more risky.

A common way of repaying an interest-only mortgage is with a **Personal Equity Plan** (Pep). Peps are dealt with in greater detail later in the book but basically allow every UK citizen to invest up to £9,000 each in shares or bonds with the income and capital gains rolling up free of income or capital gains tax.

Lenders offering interest-only mortgages will expect bor-rowers to arrange life assurance as well. This is another benefit for consumers. Instead of accepting the life assurance included in an endowment mortgage, interest-only borrowers can shop around for the best deal and premiums can vary by as much as 50 per cent.

Other options include borrowing on a **fixed** or **discounted** mortgage rate. Most lenders offer such deals to first-time buyers or people **remortgaging**, that is, changing the terms of a loan on an existing property. A fixed-rate loan has the advan-tage of having the same repayments each month. This can be a blessing when it comes to monthly budgeting. Fixed rates can last for as little as 12 months up to ten years. The shorter the period, the cheaper the rate.

The same applies to discount mortgages. These give bor-rowers a cheap-rate deal for a limited period. Typically lenders will offer anything up to 5 per cent off their standard variable rate, currently 7.49 per cent for most lenders. Again the shorter the period, the bigger the discount.

Both fixed-rate and discount deals should be viewed with some suspicion. They are loss leaders for many lenders desperate to expand their market share. While their headline rates look attractive the loans' small print can be full of nasty surprises. The biggest pitfall is the rate on offer when the term of the special deal ends. Borrowers are suddenly switched to a much higher rate, which can prove a sudden and unwelcome extra expense. Special-deal mortgages can also have heavy penalties if redeemed early when a borrower moves home.

MUTUALS

The key words are qualifying members. Not all building society savers or borrowers are able to vote or qualify for a bonus in a takeover

These have been around for hundreds of years – but have rarely been in the news as much as today. There are three main types of mutuals: insurance companies, friendly societies and building societies. It is the latter that have been grabbing the headlines.

The reason is simple. Mutuals have no shareholders and are effectively owned by their members – savers and borrowers for building societies and with-profits policyholders for insurers. If the mutual wants to change its status – by turning into a public limited company or merging with a rival – it has to have the approval of its owner/members. Recent years have shown that many are prepared to pay for this approval.

The trend began when Abbey National decided to convert from building society to bank, handing out free shares to customers along the way. Cheltenham & Gloucester Building Society members also shared a bonanza when it was taken over by Lloyds Bank, and members of the combined Halifax/Leeds group are also due windfall profits when it goes public in 1996.

The key words in the mutual debate are **qualifying members**. Not all savers or borrowers at a building society, for example, will be able to vote or qualify for a bonus or share gift in takeovers or mergers. Qualifying members are defined in these cases by the Building Societies Act. In general they include people who have been members for at least two years and have savings of more than £100.

Cheltenham & Gloucester's bonus payment scheme was hit by arguments over whether long-term savers who had changed accounts within the two-year period would qualify for bonuses – many did not – and whether people who changed joint-named accounts into their own names when their husbands died would qualify for bonuses – many did, but only after Lloyds Bank put extra money on the table for extra payments.

The picture is more cloudy when it comes to mutual insurance companies and friendly societies. The big mutuals include Standard Life, Scottish Widows, Scottish Provident and Equitable Life. They say their policyholders are better off than those of shareholder-owned insurers, as investment profits are all shared between with-profits policyholders rather than being siphoned off to pay dividends. If a mutual insurer were to decide to go public it would probably have to follow the lead of building societies and offer incentives to its policyholders.

$\mathcal{N}$ is for:

NATIONAL DEBT

In January 1995 a Devon widow left instructions in her will for the disposal of her £2m fortune. Her surviving relatives received just £2,000. The rest went to HM Treasury. It was the woman's last wish that her fortune should go to help repay the national debt – the total amount borrowed by successive governments that is still outstanding. Her generous gesture was, sadly, little more than that. For £2m would barely scratch the surface of the national debt, which is a mountainous £300bn. Indeed, just the interest payment due on this debt in the 1994–95 financial year was £22bn, equivalent to £60.3m a day, which means the £2m gift from the Devon widow would have serviced the interest on the national debt for 48 minutes.

Why is the government debt so big, where has it come from and who has lent the government the money?

To answer the last question first, much of the government's borrowing is financed by you and me. At the end of March 1995, outstanding government debt stood at £297bn. This was split up into four main types of debt. These are as follows:

1. **Gilts** Gilts are government bonds and there was £221bn worth of gilts in issue at the end of March 1995, equivalent to 74.5 per cent of the national debt.

2. **National Savings** The share of the national debt accounted for by investments in National Savings was 17.5 per cent or £53bn.
3. **Net foreign currency** £16bn or 5.3 per cent of the national debt was in the form of these bonds issued abroad.
4. **Treasury bills** These are issued by the government to fund very short-term borrowings in the City of London and accounted for 2.7 per cent or £8bn of national debt.

The first two types of debt, gilts and National Savings, will be familiar to many people. Although most gilts are held directly by insurance funds and pension funds the money used to buy them are, of course, individual's savings placed in these funds. National Savings is exclusively used by members of the public to save money. The cash deposited here through the Post Office is simply another way of lending money to the government which pays interest in return. The latter two types of debt are purely for big financial institutions and are of no interest here.

Although £297bn might sound a lot it is in fact equivalent to about 44 per cent of the country's **gross domestic product (GDP)** – a measure of our economic activity. This is much less than some European countries and significantly lower than it has been in the past. The debt has mounted up over decades and even centuries of successive government borrowing programmes. Some debt is repaid when it matures. Most, though, is refinanced either by persuading people to continue borrowing at the same or different rates or by simply repaying one debt and borrowing some more from another source.

Ever since 1694 (the year the Bank of England was formed) governments have borrowed money. In the first place this was to finance wars. From the end of World War II government borrowing has been used to finance spending on more constructive things such as the welfare state. World War II forced the national debt to within 200 per cent of GDP. Before that, events such as the American War of Independence and the Napoleonic Wars had raised it to more than 100 per cent of

GDP, as did the government's compensation to slave owners in the 1840s. The alternative to government borrowing is taxation, introduced on a wide scale when income tax was brought in permanently in 1842.

Since the high borrowings of World War II the national debt has been reduced through economic growth, inflation, the proceeds of privatisations and tax revenues outstripping government spending at various stages. In 1989 the national debt came down to £170bn, thanks largely to the 1980s boom. The government at this stage was enjoying a **public sector debt repayment (PSDR)**, the opposite of the more familiar **public sector borrowing requirement (PSBR)**. A PSDR means the flow of new debt needed by the government has dried up. In fact, tax revenues were more than spending requirements, which meant the government could start paying off the national debt, a dream of many past governments going back to Walpole in the early 1700s.

In the late boom optimism of March 1989 economists were predicting that Chancellor of the Exchequer Nigel Lawson could repay one-sixth of the then £170bn national debt within three years. But within a couple of years of enjoying a surplus in the government accounts of £14bn we were back to a PSBR of nearly £50bn by 1992, reflecting a massive swing in the UK's economic fortunes. In other words, we had gone from boom to bust, another recession was upon us, and tax revenues were therefore down but spending on unemployment benefits and other hand-outs was up.

Now the new flow of debt each year as counted by the PSBR is down to about £30bn and has been forecast by the Tories to be back to a PSDR by 1998–99.

NATIONAL INSURANCE CONTRIBUTIONS

Everyone gets a National Insurance number as a 16th birthday present from the Department of Social Security. From then on they have to pay NI contributions unless they earn less than

Everyone gets a National Insurance number as a 16th birthday present from the Department of Social Security

£58 a week. If they earn more than that they have to pay 2 per cent of the first £61 and 10 per cent of the rest up to a weekly earnings threshold of £440 (£22,880 a year). The money raised by National Insurance goes to pay for a variety of state benefits administered by the DSS. The most important one is the state pension. There are four basic classes of NI contributions:

1. **Class 1** By far the most common type of NI payment, it is paid by employees and their employers. The former pays

primary contributions based on a percentage of earnings; the latter pays **secondary contributions** also based on a percentage of employees' earnings. Employers are usually allowed to deduct Class 1 contributions from taxable profits. Once earnings reach the £22,880 threshold, employees do not need to make any further contributions but employers have to make payments based on total earnings.

Some employers reduce their total contributions by paying employees perks and other benefits in lieu of salary. However, recent rule changes have substantially reduced the employer's freedom to pay non-cash bonuses in this way. Loopholes plugged so far have included the payment to employees of precious metals, diamonds, exotic carpets, vintage cars, fine wines and coffee beans. Until April 1991 company cars used for private purposes were not counted as income when calculating Class 1 NI contribution levels. Since then, income tax benefit calculations have affected Class 1 contributions for directors or more highly paid employees who use company cars outside work.

2. **Class 2** This type of NI contribution and the two that follow are all paid by the self-employed. Class 2 is a flat-rate contribution.
3. **Class 3** This is a voluntary flat-rate contribution made by non-employed to secure social security benefits for which they would not otherwise qualify.
4. **Class 4** This is an additional NI contribution that self-employed people are obliged to pay and is based on a percentage of taxable profits.

NATIONAL SAVINGS

Ever since 1861 the public has been asked to lend the government small amounts of money through their savings to boost the nation's coffers. National Savings gives the government a convenient way of doing this from private investors. The products offered by National Savings come in the form of **savings accounts** or **fixed term investment bonds** sold through **post offices** and are considered a risk-free way of investing for income or growth.

The idea of a government-backed saving scheme was the brain child of Lord Palmerston's government which launched the Post Office Savings Bank. The then Chancellor of the Exchequer, William Gladstone, soon realised that the deposits could be used to finance government business as well as to encourage thrift among ordinary wage earners.

The most recent figures show £53bn is held in National Savings. The most popular National Savings products at the moment are **Premium Bonds**, which had August 1995 sales of £125m. The maximum Premium Bond payout was raised to a monthly £1m jackpot in December 1993 to combat the National Lottery, since when Premium Bond sales have amounted to £3bn – more than were sold in the whole of the previous ten years. There are also 350,000 smaller prizes each month ranging from £100,000 down to £100.

In addition to Premium Bonds, there are the following National Savings products:

- Five-year **Savings Certificates**, which are free of **income** and **capital gains tax**, and are available in two issues: the **9th Index-Linked** issue, which pays 2.5 per cent per year compound plus the rate of inflation if held for five years; and the ordinary **43rd** issue, which pays 5.35 per cent per year compound if held for five years.
- People under 21 can save through the **Children's Bonus Bond** issue H, which pays 6.75 per cent per year tax free if held for five years.
- **First Option Bonds** pay 6.25 per cent gross plus a 0.25 per cent bonus on investments of £20,000 and over, but basic-rate tax is deducted at source. Returns are fixed for one year at a time.
- The **Capital Bond** series 3 pays a guaranteed 6.65 per cent

gross per year if held for five years. Returns from Capital Bonds are taxable but are paid out in full without tax deducted at source.

- A similar tax treatment applies to **Pensioners Bonds** and **Income Bonds**. Anyone over 65 can buy Pensioners Bonds, which pay 7 per cent gross, fixed for five years and paid monthly. Income Bonds currently pay 6.25 per cent gross on investments of under £25,000 and 6.5 per cent on £25,000 and over. These rates are variable and distribute income monthly.

- As well as Savings Certificates and various investment bonds, National Savings offers two bank accounts: the **Investment Account** and the **Ordinary Account**. The Investment Account pays between 5 per cent and 5.75 per cent depending on the size of investment. The interest rate can vary and is taxable, but is paid gross. The Ordinary Account pays between 1.75 per cent and 2.75 per cent, with the first £70 of interest free of income tax.

Investors like National Savings because they are guaranteed by the government. Conversely, the products are not necessarily the most competitive on the market, and investors can lose out if they buy fixed rate bonds but then see interest rates rise.

NEW ISSUES

This term is most commonly applied to the shares issued by companies joining the stock market for the first time. It may also refer to subsequent share issues by companies that are already quoted on the stock market.

New shares are issued in order to raise extra capital, either to repay existing company debts, or to fund further expansion of the business. Sometimes these shares are **placed** with existing clients of the stockbrokers involved in the flotation. But, some stock market debutants will also make an **offer for sale** of at least a proportion of the shares to the general public.

At the moment, all issues above a certain size must include a public offer. But the Stock Exchange is considering a change to its listing rules that would remove this requirement.

Details of a new share issue are published in a **prospectus**. This is a brochure whose function is partly to market the shares to potential investors and partly to fulfil statutory obligations. These include the provision of specific information about the company, the background to the issue and the appropriate risk warnings. Details of larger issues may be published in newspaper advertisements, called **tombstones**.

Ever since the success of the great privatisations of the 1980s, small investors have loved new issues. This enthusiasm has been fuelled in part by the simplicity of the application process and also by memories of the instant profits enjoyed by investors in BT, British Gas and other early issues. City advisers to the first privatisations knew they had to attract to large numbers of people who had hitherto looked no further than the nearest branch of Abbey National when seeking a home for their spare cash. So the process had to be as simple as possible. All that applicants were required to do was to fill in a simple form at the back of the prospectus, or newspaper advertisement, state how many shares they wished to buy and send off a cheque for the appropriate amount. City advisers to big-name private-sector debutants such as TSB and Laura Ashley wasted no time in copying the lavish campaigns employed in successful privatisation issues.

The instant profits encouraged the practice of **stagging** – buying shares in a flotation issue with the intention of selling them immediately they come to market, rather than investing for the long term. One of the more unfortunate legacies of this populist approach was a general willingness among novices to pile into high-risk shares that were completely inappropriate for the inexperienced investor. In recent years, most new issues have been sold via placings, rather than offers for sale, as companies tired of having to deal with legions of small shareholders, rather than a few institutions.

Evidence of how risky newly floated companies can be was

provided in abundance in 1994. Virtually every new issue went to a premium, but many then proceeded to get into difficulties. The most spectacular flop was Aerostructures Hamble, whose chairman is Lord King, former chairman and now president of British Airways. Floated in May, it issued not one, but two profit warnings just five months later.

Similarly, those who rushed to buy shares in many of the new investment trusts launched during that year have since watched the value of their investment remain unchanged or, in some cases, actually fall. This is why many experienced investment-trust watchers rarely go for a new issue but wait until the shares have started trading on the stock market, when it is often possible to pick up the shares at a discount against their new issue price.

NOMINEE ACCOUNTS

These are accounts set up by stockbrokers to hold shares on behalf of private investors. Shareholders are being forced to use them as a result of big changes to the way the stock market is organised, but some investors fear they will lose out as a result.

People who buy shares must pay for them within five working days under the stock market settlement regime called **rolling settlement**. When selling shares they have five working days to hand over the share certificates. Before five-day settlement was introduced people had ten days in which to settle and were able to meet this longer deadline by sending cheques or certificates through the post. But under the five-day rule this is more difficult. Moreover the stock market plans to move to a three-day settlement period, thus putting further pressure on private investors. In order to comply with these tougher deadlines stockbrokers are telling investors to hold their shares in a stockbroker's nominee account. They can then be transferred to the new owner's nominee account within the settlement deadline.

At the same time the stock market intends to abolish the use of share certificates, known as **paper-based trading**, and record the details of trades and individuals' shareholdings electronically. This electronic share settlement is being introduced through a computer system called **Crest**. To settle share trades through Crest, investors must be prepared to hold shares in a nominee account. Shareholders' names will no longer appear on a company's share register. Instead there will simply be the number or name of the stockbroker's nominee account.

By signing over shares into a nominee account, however, investors are giving up **legal ownership and possession** of the shares, although they retain **beneficial ownership**. This has raised concerns that in some cases investors will be blocked from receiving company accounts, shareholder perks, the right to attend company meetings, and even dividends.

To answer shareholder fears **ProShare**, the wider share ownership lobby group, has published a voluntary code of conduct for nominees and quoted companies. The code demands that companies make sure investors on their register represented by nominees receive free copies of accounts, and have access to shareholder meetings with the opportunity to vote by proxy. It also requires a statement of how much a nominee service costs and assurances about security arrangements. Monies placed into a nominee on the advice of a stockbroker are protected under the Investors Compensation Scheme. This means that up to £48,000 of an investor's holding in a nominee company may be returned if a stockbroker perpetrates a fraud.

O is for:

OCCUPATIONAL PENSION SCHEMES

Some 11 million people, or virtually half the workforce, are members of company pension schemes. Around six million retired people receive payments from a company scheme. There are two main types: **final salary (or earnings-related) schemes** and **money purchase (or defined contributions) schemes**.

With the former type, both employee and employer pay contributions into the fund. The benefits depend on the number of years the pensioner has been a member of the scheme in relation to the salary paid in the year, or years, leading up to retirement, although the relevant earnings may be those of a few years earlier if they were higher. Depending on the scheme, you will normally receive either half, or two-thirds of final earnings as a pension, although full benefits will probably depend on 40 years' membership. You may be able to choose whether you convert part of the benefits into a **tax-free lump sum,** or will automatically be paid a lump sum as part of your retirement benefit.

With money purchase schemes, contributions will again be made by both employer and employee. These, plus any invest-ment gains, will build up to an individual fund on retirement from which the pension will be paid. Part of this fund will be paid in the form of a tax-free lump sum, and the rest will normally be used to buy an annuity. The employer usually pays administration charges.

Some schemes are **contracted out** of the **state earnings-related pension scheme (Serps)**, which means that both employers and employees make lower National Insurance contributions. If it is contracted in, employees receive Serps as well as the company pension. Members of occupational schemes can also make **additional voluntary contributions (AVCs)** within the company scheme, up to Inland Revenue limits, to top up their final benefits. Alternatively, scheme members may choose to make **free-standing AVCs** through insurance companies, building societies and other outside providers.

Members changing jobs have three choices: they may leave the money to continue growing in their old scheme; transfer it to the new company scheme; or transfer it into a personal pension plan. The **transfer value** is calculated by the actuary of the old scheme.

Occupational pension schemes were once seen as the safest and best way to save for your retirement. Sadly this image took a hammering because of the Mirror Group pension scandal where hundreds of millions of pounds of present and future pensioners' money were found to be missing from the company's pension fund.

As a result of this catastrophe the government set up the Goode committee in June 1992, which was given the job of discovering how pensions law could be improved. The committee's recommendations led to the introduction of a bill into the Houses of Parliament that eventually became the **Pensions Act 1995**. This was an attempt to paper over the cracks in pensions legislation and consumer protection that had allowed the Mirror Group money to seep out. The Act's main aims are to improve the way pension schemes are administered and run and to ensure greater security of members' benefits. The Act creates such bodies as the Occupational Pensions Regulatory Authority to supervise the new system of rules.

OFFICE OF FAIR TRADING (OFT)

As the name suggests, this is the body responsible for protecting consumers and encouraging competition. It is a government department founded in 1973 and is headed by a **director-general** (John Bridgeman). Its main objective is to promote and safeguard the interests of consumers. The OFT has statutory duties arising from 20 items of legislation. These duties mean the OFT is charged with keeping the UK market for goods and services under review in order to identify and tackle trading practices of all kinds that may adversely affect consumers' interests. This can mean intervening over the practices of a whole sector of industry or commerce, or in the activities of a single trader which mislead or deceive customers.

Not surprisingly the business world sometimes sees the OFT as an ill-informed busybody. It investigates possible abuses arising from monopolies, anti-competitive practices, mergers and restrictive trade practices. Naturally its influence depends on the attitude of the government of the day, or, more specifically, on the attitude of the Cabinet minister responsible for trade and industry. He or she may feel that the OFT is perhaps being overzealous in pursuit of its aims and may therefore choose to ignore its referrals and recommendations.

As far as family finance is concerned the OFT can be regularly heard criticising the insurance industry for anti-competitive practices damaging to consumers' interests. It has investigated such things as:

- endowment policies;
- Crest, the new electronic share transfer system;
- prepaid funeral plans;
- mortgage lenders and advisers;
- unfair clauses in insurance policies;
- the sale of private medical insurance and travel insurance;
- credit cards; and
- moneylenders.

OFFSHORE INVESTMENTS

United Kingdom-based taxpayers can delay paying income and capital gains tax by placing money offshore

For many people, offshore investing conjures up images of shady dealings practised by tycoons and wealthy individuals with something to hide. True, many offshore centres cater for this trade – mainly for tax purposes – particularly those island nations that service the millionaires and billionaires of the United States. But the UK has its very own offshore satellites that provide perfectly legal and safe havens for taxpayers and investors who require something a little different.

The main offshore centres for UK residents are **Jersey, Guernsey,** the **Isle of Man** and **Bermuda.** All these are recognised by the British government and hold **designated territory status,** which means that their systems of financial regulation and investor protection are considered to be at least as good as that offered by our own Financial Services Act. These offshore centres offer investment funds such as unit trusts and investment trusts, bank and building society savings accounts and life assurance.

Why, though, should a UK resident want to put money offshore? There are two reasons: **tax** and **investment freedom.** Offshore tax havens carry much mystery and myth. It is true that UK-based taxpayers can delay paying income and capital gains tax by placing money offshore. This is known as **tax avoidance** and is perfectly legal, but the Inland Revenue does expect to see tax paid on this money eventually. Income is income as far as the Revenue is concerned, regardless of where it comes from.

Offshore-based savings and investments pay interest and investment income gross, that is, without tax deducted at source. This means UK residents receive a one-off boost to their cash flows, and it also allows them to sort out their own tax affairs. Depending on when interest is credited to an offshore bank or building society account it is sometimes possible for UK residents to defer paying income tax for between 18 months and two years.

The big advantage of offshore unit trusts is their ability to accumulate gains tax-free within the fund. Such **accumulation funds** pay no income. A tax liability arises when investors repatriate the assets to the UK where gains are taxed as income not capital. This means investors can enjoy growth that compounds gross before paying tax and can defer that tax bill for several years. A common tax avoidance ploy might be for a UK resident to invest in an offshore accumulator fund, enjoy gross returns and then repatriate the money when they are in a lower tax bracket, possibly after retiring.

People who intend to retire abroad can also use offshore accumulator funds to place long-term savings outside the UK tax net. Moreover these funds are useful parking places for assets during periods of political uncertainty or higher tax rates.

The other type of offshore unit trusts are **distributor funds**. These must pay out 85 per cent of their income as dividends, which are taxable. Any other profits are taxed as capital gains.

Most big UK building societies have offshore subsidiaries, which are guaranteed by their onshore parents. In the Isle of Man there is an added layer of security in the form of a depositors' protection scheme covering banks and building societies. The other offshore centres rely on a screening process to weed out weak or unreliable institutions. Financial advisers and insurance salesmen based in the UK who sell offshore-based products must comply with the sales and marketing requirements of the Financial Services Act.

OMBUDSMEN

The financial ombudsman's role is to act as an independent arbitrator when disputes between personal finance companies and their disgruntled customers reach an impasse. Most, but not all, areas of the financial services industry are covered by one or other of the ombudsman schemes, although the lines between them are sometimes blurred and it is not always clear which case should be dealt with by which ombudsman. The public are not charged for the service, which is only available for cases that have not been through the courts.

Ombudsmen are paid for by the financial services companies that are members of each individual ombudsman scheme. Membership is optional. Some cynical observers say that not all ombudsmen are as successful as they ought to be in resisting pressure from their memberships, although this is hotly denied by both parties. Where a case falls outside the ombudsmen's remit, the aggrieved customer has no alternative but to take the company with whom he or she is in dispute to court, or try to get their case dealt with directly by the appropriate regulatory body. It is worth remembering that many such cases will fall within the remit of the small claims court, which is much cheaper than the alternatives.

The **Personal Investment Authority (PIA) Ombudsman** considers complaints about the marketing of investment products and administrative matters. While all PIA members must submit to scrutiny of their marketing methods, any agreement to having administration probed is voluntary. Where members do not agree to scrutiny of complaints about administration, these cases will normally be passed on to the insurance ombudsman. If it is not clear which is the relevant ombudsman for your case, try the PIA first. You will then be referred on to the appropriate scheme.

The **Insurance Ombudsman** looks at complaints about general insurance, plus any life assurance gripes not covered by the PIA. Occasionally, he or she will adjudicate on a pensions matter, but these are more commonly dealt with by the PIA and pensions ombudsmen. He or she cannot look at bonuses, surrender values or at cases in which the insurer in question is not the complainant's own.

The **Building Societies Ombudsman** covers matters involving mortgages, savings and banking services, including maladministration and bad advice. All societies belong to the scheme, but have the right to reject the ombudsman's findings within 28 days of the complainants' decision to accept them.

The **Banking Ombudsman** may only investigate complaints not covered by the Financial Services Act. Areas covered include 'phantom' cash withdrawals, credit and debit cards, loans, bank charges and foreign currency. Some complaints from third parties are accepted, such as where cheque guarantee cards have not been honoured.

The **Investment Ombudsman** covers investment matters that do not come within the remit of other ombudsmen. He or she considers cases involving members of the Investment

Managers Regulatory Organisation (Imro). If they are also members of the PIA, the complaint may have to be considered by the PIA ombudsman, depending on the circumstances. Matters involving stockbrokers normally come under the arbitration scheme run by the Securities and Futures Authority.

The **Pensions Ombudsman** looks after occupational pensions and some queries concerning personal pensions, mainly to do with administration errors, but does not consider state schemes. Complainants must first contact the Occupational Pensions Advisory Service (Opas).

The **Inland Revenue Adjudicator** considers most complaints concerning personal taxation, including overpayments and the behaviour of Revenue staff. He or she cannot look at any problems to do with tax law. The first port of call is the local tax office.

OPEN-ENDED INVESTMENT COMPANIES

Over the past 60 years millions of savers have put what now amounts to £160bn into two types of collective investment schemes: **unit trusts** and **investment trusts**. Bought for their convenience and low risk, these vehicles have served the needs of savers well over the years. Yet this multibillion pound market is about to undergo the biggest changes seen for many years, according to the Securities and Investments Board, the chief regulatory authority that covers family finance issues.

You will be excused for feeling a little puzzled by such a statement. If this is so important why haven't you heard about it before? For such an important development in such a big market there doesn't seem to be much fuss.

The fact of the matter is that the shake-up has not resulted from any consumer pressure group or financial scandal but from special pleading by the unit trust industry. It has persuaded **Her Majesty's Treasury** – the ultimate financial services power in the land – to license a new type of collective investment vehicle called the **open-ended investment company**. The new open-ended investment company (oeic – pronounced 'oik' – although an alternative is being sought by the Treasury) will replace the **unit trust** as the most common form of collective investment vehicle.

As the name suggests, an oeic is a company as opposed to a trust. Instead of trustees an oeic will have a board of directors to oversee the proper running of the investment company. Oeics will issue shares instead of units and the price of these shares will be shown as a single, mid-market price, compared to the dual buy-and-sell prices shown by unit trusts.

Anyone who has read the section on **investment trusts** may be forgiven for thinking that oeics are a very similar creature. However, despite the corporate trappings such as shares and boards of directors, oeics are very definitely the close cousins of unit trusts not investment trusts. In fact, the crucial difference between oeics and investments trusts is the term 'open-ended'.

Investment trusts issue a set number of shares as does any quoted company. By issuing these shares the investment trust raises a specific amount of money or capital and is said to be **closed-ended** as a result. The price of an investment trust's shares depends on the demand for them in the stock market. Little or no demand means that share prices perform badly and may not reflect the performance of the trust's assets being invested by the fund manager. They are said to be **undervalued** and at a **discount** to the value of the trust's asset.

Oeics, on the other hand, can issue shares on demand, there is no limit. The price of the shares is determined by dividing the assets of the company by the number of shares in issue. The shares will always reflect the value of the assets, so there is no question of them trading at a discount.

Why, then, have oeics been given the go-ahead now? The answer lies in Europe. Oeics have been invented mainly to help UK-based investment management companies that run unit trusts compete on the Continent. Investors in France and Germany for instance are used to the oeic-type structure and are not familiar with the concept of trusts and trustees. They prefer to deal with a corporate structure.

The benefits to British investors, the people likely to be most affected, have been treated as something of a side issue compared to the commercial interests of the investment management groups. Happily for all concerned there are one or two beneficial spin-offs for customers who put their money into oeics, although they are few and far between.

The trouble with unit trusts is that they are too complicated for most people to understand, especially foreigners – or so the investment management companies in the City of London argue. They have therefore lobbied the Treasury long and hard for a new product that they can sell more easily both abroad and at home. Without oeics the £113bn which is run by UK-based unit trust managers would be re-registered in more liberal offshore centres such as Dublin, resulting in job losses for London, Edinburgh and other domestic financial centres, says the City.

But what does all this special pleading by the unit trust industry mean for consumers? Many existing unit trust investors will see their holdings decanted into new oeics with identical investment objectives. These can then be rebranded and repackaged and promoted abroad and at home. New investors should find the same range of investments available to them and may even find oeics a little simpler to understand, but they are likely to be confused by the continued existence of unit trusts, which will still be run alongside oeics under the existing rules and regulations by some managers.

Assuming, therefore, that oeics do take precedence, what are the advantages, and why get rid of good old unit trusts? According to experts the change from unit trust to oeics will not make any difference to investment performance. It may, however, make new funds cheaper to set up, with charges that will be easier to understand. Funds are also likely to be better designed, with the needs of the consumer more in mind.

At present unit trusts have complicated charging and

pricing systems. Managers quote an **initial charge** in sales literature but the real price is higher because of the trust's **bid offer spread**. This spread between the prices at which units can be bought and sold reflect costs such as stamp duty and the bid offer spreads on the underlying shares. The unit trust's bid offer spread can move unexpectedly if there are large numbers of buyers or sellers in a unit trust.

By contrast, oeics will quote one buying and one selling price set at the mid-market price for the oeic shares. The fans of oeics claim that people do not understand dual pricing, that is, quoting a price at which you buy and a price at which you sell – although such a dual price system has never stopped holidaymakers buying foreign currency!

The other advantage of oeics is product design. Investment companies should be able to design funds which better meet consumers' needs. The shares issued by oeics may well have different levels of charges depending on how they are sold. Shares bought direct will have low charges while the charges for shares bought through financial advisers will be higher to cover commission. Shares could be denominated in different currencies to benefit investors who take a strong view on currency trends. A further possibility is the introduction of limited issue funds. This would be an oeic that is open to new money for a specific period, say, a month, and then closes its doors for three or six months. By doing this the fund managers will be able to offer specific short-term guarantees that will be attractive to the more cautious investor.

Many unit trust investors will see their funds converted into oeics as fund managers try to boost their businesses by adopting this new vehicle. But unit holders will get a say in this process if people representing 1 per cent of the trust's assets or at least 25 unit holders ask for a vote to be taken. If so, then a simple majority of those voting would be required for the conversion to go ahead. If the vote is in favour, the trust's assets will be transferred into the oeic. So an investor with 1,000 units with a bid price of £1 each will probably see the holding transferred into, say, 1,000 oeic shares at £1 each, or maybe 2,000 shares at 50p each or some such equivalent. Investors will not face a tax liability and the unit trust company will take care of the paperwork.

The Treasury assures consumers that they will not lose any rights to protection under the Financial Services Act by converting to an oeic and that the investors' compensation scheme will still be available to them.

OVERSEAS STOCK MARKETS

Before the start of the 1980s, investing money anywhere other than Britain was considered highly unusual. Investors big and small – be they insurance or pension funds or individuals – would stick to what they knew best, UK equities.

Over the past 20 years, however, horizons have widened, helped in no small part by the lifting of exchange controls by Margaret, now Baroness, Thatcher. This allowed investors freedom to move their capital around the world's markets. The only penalty they had to watch out for was the impact of adverse currency movements on the burgeoning foreign exchange markets. Thus, free to move money around the globe, investors soon found themselves buying shares on Wall Street. Later the more adventurous started to buy into the Tokyo stock market (now considered to be one of the world's most important), up to the present day when few countries have been left untried by the British investor.

The 1980s saw the rise of the **emerging markets**. These are the stock markets of countries whose economies are emerging from years of economic slumber generally caused by political instability or prolonged dictatorships. Latin and Central America as well as the Far Eastern economies are the classic emerging markets. The Far Eastern markets have been nicknamed the 'Tiger Economies' because of their fast economic growth and highly performing stock markets. The newest recruits to the ranks of emerging markets are the states of the former Soviet Union, the Middle East – most notably Lebanon – and Africa.

Nowadays, no big institutional investor is without exposure to overseas markets to provide diversity to large portfolios. This means investors do not have to rely on just one market for their returns, and this accordingly helps to reduce risk.

The best way for individuals to gain access to overseas markets is through unit or investment trusts. These trusts cover all possible angles from Latin American bond funds to Asian equity funds. African and Middle Eastern funds have also started to be launched, although these at present are for the more sophisticated.

OVER-THE-COUNTER MARKETS

In the financial world, over-the-counter (OTC) markets exist for any securities or investments that are not bought and sold through an exchange. In Britain the main OTC market exists for the complex **derivative** products sold by investment banks to big institutional investors such as pension funds and insurers.

This market has been the cause for concern among central banks around the world, which are responsible for regulating their various financial systems. The OTC market in derivatives-based securities is said by critics to lack transparency. No one knows what exposure any one institution may have to other counter-parties in the market. If one should fail to meet its obligations under the terms of a contract this could have a domino effect, causing others to default and, ultimately, financial catastrophe and meltdown. This danger is known as **systemic risk**.

There was an OTC market for UK company shares but this died an ignominious death in September 1988 when the leading player, Harvard Securities, was refused authorisation under the Financial Services Act. The OTC market for shares fell outside the Stock Exchange's authority and was peopled by hard-sell dealers looking for private clients who would be willing to take a gamble on speculative companies marketing things such as customised horoscopes and cures for stretch marks. At its height the market traded the shares of 160 companies and claimed to have a market value of £660m.

The problem with many OTC markets is a lack of information about prices and company values as well as clear regulation. Investors must rely on the dealers for reliable buying and selling data, which means that the potential for abuse is huge.

$\mathcal{P}$ is for:

PERKS

Several companies offer perks to some, if not all, their shareholders. One of the best known is P&O, the shipping and construction company, whose generous channel ferry travel concessions are thought to account for the unusually large number of private shareholders on its register. Others offer books of money-off vouchers, or a one-off discount every year. The more generous companies provide a set discount on all purchases, or those made in a specific area of the business. A wide range of goods and services is available, from cars, clothing and credit cards, to wines and washing machines.

No one should invest in a company solely for the perks. Investment performance is more important than a matching set of socks and underpants, or a weekend in Bournemouth. But they undoubtedly enhance the attractions of shares that are in any case considered by the experts to be worth a gamble – and they can add to the warm glow of ownership enjoyed when visiting a member of a store, restaurant or hotel chain in which you have a stake.

Stockbrokers' nominee accounts can sometimes cause difficulties for people whose investment portfolios include share perks. Some companies will not supply the extra benefits to

SHAREHOLDER PERKS		
Company	Perk	Minimum Holding
Kwik-Fit	10% off two £10+ purchases	100 shares
Thorntons	£21 vouchers off sweets	200 shares
Sketchley	25% off dry cleaning	1000 shares
Austin Reed	15% discounts	500 shares
Burton Group	12.5% discounts to £625	5000 shares
Laura Ashley	15% off one purchase	None
Moss Bros	10% discounts	250 shares
Next	25% one-off discount	500 shares
Sears	£500 of vouchers	500 shares
Iceland	Food vouchers	None
Airtours	10% discount on hols	None
Brit Airways	10% coupon off flight	200 shares
P&O	Various depending on hdg	Varies
Rank Org	15% discount on hols	Any held 2 yrs
Trafalgar House	10 to 15% off Cunard hols	500/1000 shares
Greene King	15 to 20% wine discounts	None
Whitbread	Various	None
Forte Htls	10% discount	300 shares
Quns Mt Hses	Various	None
Savoy Grp	10% discounts	None
Asprey	15% discounts	5062 shares
McCarthy & Stone	£1000 per property	500 shares
Harry Ramsden's	20% discounts	500 shares
Argos	Various one-offs	None
Boots	10 £1 vouchers	100 shares
Storehouse	10% off up to £500	500 shares

shareholders in nominee accounts. Alternatively, stockbrokers may refuse to accept the extra hassle involved in sharing these perks, or even retain them for their own use rather than passing them on to nominee clients.

PERMANENT INTEREST BEARING SHARES (Pibs)

Building societies issue Pibs as a way of raising money. Although they are called shares and are listed on the stock market, Pibs work just like bonds. They pay interest half-yearly, normally at a fixed rate although one or two issues pay a variable rate of interest. The interest is paid out net, which means that non-taxpayers must claim tax back from the Revenue while higher rate taxpayers must declare a further tax liability.

When buying Pibs you are in effect lending money to the building society, which pays you interest in return. Pibs are more risky than a building society's savings accounts and thus pay higher interest to compensate. In the unlikely event of a building society going bust, holders of Pibs would have to wait in line behind all other creditors before getting a payout.

Because Pibs pay higher than normal levels of interest they appeal to people looking for income. The gross yields from Pibs are very attractive. There are 18 issues from such well-known names as Bradford & Bingley, Halifax and the Leeds Permanent. With the exception of one Halifax issue, all yield more than 10 per cent, with most above 10.5 per cent. Pibs must be bought through a stockbroker although some societies are considering selling the shares over the counter in their branches. Another attraction of Pibs is the relatively low minimum investment. There are plenty of issues with a £1,000 minimum although Bradford & Bingley requires £10,000, and Leeds Permanent and the Halifax require £50,000.

Unlike most bonds, Pibs do not have a maturity date at which the investments are redeemed by building societies and original capital paid back. This lack of a repayment date means investors who want to retrieve their capital have to sell the shares on the stock market through a stockbroker. This can be risky, especially if you are forced into a quick sale. There is no guarantee that the price you receive on selling Pibs will be higher than the price you paid. You could therefore end up losing money as a result and eating into capital. The price of Pibs depends largely on interest rates and also on the credit worthiness of the issuing building society.

If interest rates rise, savings accounts become more attractive while the more risky Pibs become less so. Their price falls as a result. If interest rates fall, the opposite happens. If a building society publishes a poor set of financial results which shows a big rise in bad debts, then the price of the society's Pibs might fall on fears for the financial strength of the society. But if people stick to the well-known names there should be no problems on this count.

The big advantage of Pibs is that they allow investors to lock into a high, fixed level of income indefinitely, which can be important when planning household budgets. Investors should remember that Pibs are not covered by the Building Societies Investor Protection Fund, which looks after deposit holders should a society fail.

PERSONAL EQUITY PLANS

These were the brainchild of Nigel, now Lord, Lawson who introduced them when Chancellor of the Exchequer in 1986. From January of the following year people were allowed to invest in shares tax free. The idea behind Personal Equity Plans (Peps) is to encourage wider share ownership and long-term personal savings. They gave everyone over the age of 18 a way of sheltering investments from both income and capital gains tax. Dividends and capital growth thus escaped the tax net although Pep contributions did not receive any up-front tax relief.

These tax breaks still stand today, but a stream of regulatory changes since 1987 has changed Peps dramatically, making them a central plank of many people's financial plans. At the outset, people were allowed to invest just £2,400 into the tax-free shelter of a Pep, making them of only marginal interest to most investors. Since then the allowance has risen through various levels and now stands at a more chunky £6,000. This is known

A self-select Pep allows investors complete freedom of choice over which investments they hold

as the **general Pep allowance.** There is also a separate Pep allowance introduced in 1992 that allows people to invest an extra £3,000 each year in the shares of a **single company.** Anyone who has invested their full Pep allowance every year including 1995–96 (including single-company Peps) will have put aside a tax-free fund invested in shares or share-based investments of £55,200 or £110,400 for a married couple.

Since Peps opened for subscription in January 1987 the Treasury has been besieged by special pleading from certain

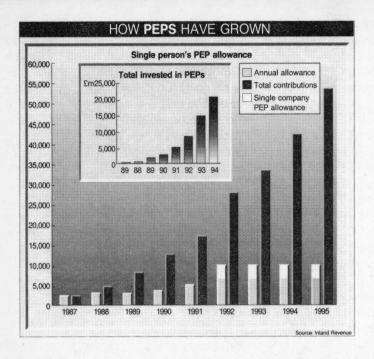

HOW **PEPS** HAVE GROWN

Single person's PEP allowance

Total invested in PEPs

- Annual allowance
- Total contributions
- Single company PEP allowance

Source: Inland Revenue

elements in the City who have tried to persuade the chancellor to widen the Pep allowance. On the whole they have succeeded. The loudest calls for change have come from **unit trust managers**. In 1987, of the £2,400 Pep allowance just £420 could be invested in a **qualifying unit trust** – that is, one that invests at least 50 per cent of its portfolio in UK or European shares.

The unit trust element has risen through £540, £2,400 and £3,000 up to the full £6,000 general Pep allowance, which was granted in the tax year 1992–93. This also applies to investment trusts. Instead of placing the full £6,000 Pep allowance in one qualifying unit trust, customers can place £1,500 of it in a **non-qualifying unit trust** – that is, one that has less than 50 per cent of its assets invested in the UK or Europe.

Peps invested in unit or investment trusts tend to be bought by people direct from fund management companies or through independent financial advisers. The drawback of this is that the Pep is tied to one trust. If a person wants to switch during the tax year to another trust run by a different fund manager he or she has to go through a complex and often costly Pep transfer process. The best way round this is to use a **self-select Pep** that allows freedom of choice over which investments they hold within their Pep tax shelter, be it shares, unit trusts or investment trusts. Many people prefer to place their Pep allowance directly in shares rather than use the often expensive services of a unit trust fund manager, and a self-select Pep is the way to do this. Self-select Peps are available off the shelf from stockbrokers and some IFAs who will levy an administration charge for the running of the plan on an investor's behalf. They will also charge their normal dealing commission for buying or selling investments.

For investors who do not wish to pick their own investments a unit or investment trust can make sense. Competition among unit trust managers has meant that charges have been forced down. Most unit trust managers now offer a Pep free of charge with their qualifying funds and in many cases the underlying unit trust charges have been reduced. Some big investment companies have started to offer unit trusts without an initial charge if bought through a Pep. They have replaced the initial charge with a sliding scale of exit charges that reduce every year the Pep is held, eventually disappearing after five years.

But investors who opt for a unit trust Pep rather than a self-select Pep should remember that no matter how cheap the unit trust Pep, it is investment performance that counts. A cheap unit trust Pep with a poor fund manager will always be beaten by a good fund manager running a fund with standard charges.

A recent change to the Pep rules announced in the 1994 Budget was the introduction of **bonds** to the list of eligible Pep investments. Bonds are fixed-interest securities issued by companies and are considered to be a less volatile, lower-risk investment than shares. Chancellor Kenneth Clarke introduced bonds to the Pep arena to try to help companies raise money from other sources apart from bank borrowing or new share issues. The introduction of bonds also has the benefit of allowing investors to diversify holdings away from shares and introduce a lower-risk element to their tax-free portfolios. Bonds are also very popular with investors seeking high income who are not too worried about capital growth. An explanation of how bonds work is given on pages 19–20.

The introduction of corporate bond Peps has accelerated the move towards low-cost Peps, with unit trust managers entering the market with bond-based schemes that have no initial or exit charges and only the slimmest of annual management charges. But again, investors are warned against buying a Pep simply because it has low charges.

Investments into a Pep must normally be made in cash – which includes cheques, standing orders and direct debits. To shelter an existing portfolio of shares inside a Pep they must be sold and then bought back within the Pep wrapper. There are, however, two exceptions to this rule:

1. Investors can transfer shares allocated in a public offer, including privatisation shares, into both general and single-company Peps – as long as they act within 42 days of obtaining the shares.
2. Investors with an approved savings-related share option scheme can transfer shares into a single-company Pep, as can people with shares from an approved profit-sharing scheme. People with shares from an executive or discretionary share option scheme must **bed-and-breakfast** their shares before placing them in a Pep.

Investors can pay into one single and one general Pep each tax year but it is possible to switch holdings in unit trust Peps from one manager to another. People are allowed to add to the same Pep, be it a general or single-company Pep, year after year, or they can take out a different Pep with a different manager in each tax year. A full or partial withdrawal from a Pep in any one tax year does not mean investors can make fresh subscriptions of the same value as the amount withdrawn. Investors can only add to their plans within a given tax year if they have subscribed less than the maximum annual allowance.

As far as cash holdings in a Pep are concerned there is no limit to the amount or length of time cash can be held in a general Pep as long as it is held to buy qualifying investments. Cash held within a single-company Pep must be invested within 42 days of receipt by the plan manager. Any interest earned on the cash held within a Pep will be free of tax unless interest of more than £180 for each plan is withdrawn in a tax year without being invested in shares, unit trusts or investment trusts.

PERSONAL PENSIONS

Personal pensions as they exist today began in 1988. Before then, people bought Section 226 policies, or retirement annuities, which are similar, but governed by different rules.

Personal pensions may be bought by any working person under 75 who is not a member of an occupational pension scheme. They are money-purchase schemes, which means that contributions build up in your own personal pension 'pot', boosted by any investment gains. On maturity, up to 25 per cent of the accumulated fund is paid as a tax-free lump sum and the rest is used to buy an **annuity** (an income for life). You can choose between the following types of scheme:

- deposit-based policies, which are similar to savings accounts;
- with-profits policies, which add non-removable **annual bonuses** during the lifetime of the policy and also pay a **terminal bonus** at the end; and
- unit-linked policies, which are riskier, but offer potentially higher returns.

Personal pensions are normally sold by insurance companies. The maximum amount you are allowed to contribute each year depends on your age, ranging from 17.5 per cent for under-35s to 40 per cent for the over-60s. Contributions are made in two different ways. You may either tie yourself to paying regular premiums into a single pension policy on a monthly, quarterly or annual basis, or contribute a series of one-off lump sums. The latter is a more flexible method as it does not tie you to any particular pension provider, so enabling you to seek out the best deal on offer at the time. The amount of income you receive from a personal pension depends on how long the money has been invested, the investment performance while it has been in the fund, the effect of charges levied on the fund, and the type of annuity you decide to buy. It will also depend on prevailing annuity rates.

Some schemes allow plan-holders to contract out of the **state earnings-related pension scheme (Serps)**, which means that the Department of Social Security makes a contribution directly into your fund. The portion of the fund containing DSS contributions is known as your **protected rights**. The decision to contract out depends on the age and sex of the individual concerned. Younger people are normally better off contracting out. Some experts, though, advise all women to remain contracted in. This is because women tend to live longer, so annuity rates are lower, whereas Serps pensions are the same for both sexes.

PET INSURANCE

Veterinary bills can run into hundreds of pounds – sometimes more than £1,000. Treatment for a broken leg can cost cat owners up to £300. For dogs, the charge for the same injury can be as much as £1,000.

Petplan, founded 19 years ago, was the first dedicated pet insurance company. Since then, a number of competitors have entered the field – though, even now, only an

The cost of fixing a broken leg for a cat can cost £300 and up to £1,000 for a dog

estimated 7 per cent of dogs, and 2 per cent of cats, are covered by pet insurance. Petplan still retains a 42 per cent market share and pays out an average £250,000 in claims each week.

Typical pet insurance policies cover vets' fees for illness and accident, but exclude vaccinations, neutering, pregnancy or chronic conditions diagnosed before cover is taken out. Other common benefits include: a lump sum payable on accidental, or premature, death; legal liability cover if your pet injures someone, or damages their property; compensation for loss through theft or straying; kennel or cattery fees if the owner has suddenly to go into hospital; and holiday cancellation fees if the pet is in need of emergency surgery. Policies for horses and ponies will normally also cover permanent loss of use, theft of or accidental damage to tack, and personal accident insurance.

Terms and conditions vary widely. Most policies impose an excess, which means you will have to pay the first part of any claim. Typically, each claim will also be capped, although limits are usually quite high. Premiums depend on level of cover and, with dogs, the breed and area you live in. Under the **Dangerous Dogs Act 1991**, owners must take out insurance against your legal liabilities if your dog attacks and injures another person. A few standard pet policies will cover this, but most will not.

PHONE BANKING

There is a popular misconception that banking by phone is most popular among people who live a long way from their local branch. Research carried out by the Co-operative Bank indicates, however, that people in remote country areas often prefer to travel to the nearest branch rather than pick up the phone. This is thought to be because country people derive pleasure from the social contact involved. Most telephone banking customers live in towns and cities, where life is normally more pressurised.

The current passion for dialling up every conceivable financial service began in the mid-1980s when Peter Woods set up **Direct Line**, the first company to sell cut-price insurance over the telephone. Various attempts were made to adapt the idea for banking customers, but the earlier services tended to involve computerised answering services and were not very user-friendly.

In 1989, Midland launched the first fully-fledged, stand-alone telephone banking service, **First Direct**, employing real human beings at the end of the phone. The new bank provided

'Is that the Phone Bank? This is a hold up!'

the blueprint for many other phone banks. Its services include setting up, changing and cancelling standing orders, bill paying, balance inquiries, and account transfers – all at local call rates. Then, in October 1994, the TSB became the first high-street bank to launch a telephone service that was fully integrated with its branch and cash machine networks. PhoneBank offers all normal services, including mortgages and home insurance quotations.

All the main high-street banks except – ironically, perhaps – Midland now offer some form of phone banking service for branch-based customers, although not all are 24-hour operations. NatWest's Primeline, set up in 1991 and offering a phone bank service to customers of its high-street branches, only operates from 8.00 a.m. to 10.00 p.m., or 9.00 a.m. to 5.00 a.m. at weekends. Barclaycall started in November 1994 and LloydsLine began operating a pilot service in 1995. The Co-op's phone banking operation became fully operational in spring 1992. In 1995, it extended the service to small businesses. It now has 1.5 million telephone customers, but offers only a limited service between midnight and 6 a.m., when a computerised voice deals with balance inquiries only.

Most banks charge calls at local rate, but Bank of Scotland's Banking Direct has a freepost and freephone service. It also offers Screenphone, a combined electronic banking screen and telephone, supplied by the bank. Banking Direct is a stand-alone operation, similar to First Direct. The BoS has another phone-banking service aimed at its branch-based customers, called PhoneLine, which takes calls at local rates. Citibank's Citiphone service may be used as a stand-alone service, or linked to customers' existing accounts. It also has a freephone number.

POUND COST AVERAGING

This is a useful side effect of regular saving that makes a virtue out of falling markets. Regular saving involves drip feeding often small amounts of money into the stock market on a monthly basis. Most regular savers invest through the monthly saving schemes offered by unit trusts and investment trusts, which invest in stock markets all over the world. The amounts saved can be small, starting at £20, with no upper limit, and these schemes can be a lot cheaper than buying shares direct each month from a stockbroker.

Imagine an investor has £10,000 to invest. He or she could put it all into the market on the same day. Buying a unit trust, for example, with units priced at £10 each, he or she would own 1,000 units. But stock markets are volatile places and share prices can fall a long way in a short space of time. The UK market enjoyed a big rally in 1995 and reached record levels. This type of thing makes a lot of investors nervous about putting more money into the market. They wait until it becomes a lot clearer what factors might move prices in the near future. If our investor decides to put money in today, he or she could easily see the market tumble soon after. Over the course of a year he or she might lose, say, 10 per cent, or £1,000, from the original investment.

The investor might be better off opting for a regular savings plan. Instead of one investment of £10,000 the investor could make 12 investments of £833, and would be buying on 12 days during the year instead of just one. As prices fall during the course of the year our regular investor would be buying more units for £10,000 through 12 monthly investments than he or she would with a one-off purchase, and might end up with, say, 1,800 units after 12 months rather than simply 1,000. Having more units to your name pays off when prices rise. The long-term effect of regular savings is to smooth out stock markets' peaks and troughs, and this is called pound cost averaging. The more volatile a stock market, the more advantageous it is to go for pound cost averaging. This is why regular savings can work so well in emerging markets.

People can link regular savings schemes to Personal Equity Plans and often find them a useful way of putting a bit aside each month for a child or grandchild.

Of course regular savings are not always better than lump sum investments. Investors who get their timing right and invest a lump sum in shares when prices are at their lowest will almost always beat the more cautious regular saver. Many people, however, do not have the time, know-how or discipline to work out when the best time is to invest, so buying shares or units on a monthly basis is a convenient way of taking the hassle out of stock-market investing.

PRIVATE BANKING

This frock coat and top hat service has its roots in the days of Jane Austen and Napoleon Bonaparte. During the first 200 years of its existence, it relied on the landed gentry and other members of the privileged classes to provide business. But, in recent years, the industry has begun to widen its net and woo people with rather less wealth and of rather lower social status.

The principal function of these banks is to assume total responsibility for the general financial affairs of those who are too busy, or too bored, to take responsibility for themselves. They offer basic banking facilities, including standing orders and direct debits, credit and debit cards and large low-interest overdrafts. Most offer £250 cheque guarantee cards, and allow customers to withdraw higher than normal amounts from cashpoint machines. Foreign exchange rates also tend to be cheaper. The most important service, however, is that of fund management, including a full, one-stop advisory service involving stockbrokers, solicitors, tax experts, family trust experts and estate planners. All give independent financial advice, which gives customers access to the best deals available on the market.

Nowadays, the industry is making a concerted effort to hoover up disenchanted high-street bank customers whose incomes and financial needs are of the type that would benefit from the personal service offered by private banks. Exclusivity and service are the two principal carrots used to entice the better-heeled high-street customer through the portals of such august names as Coutts & Co, Child & Co and C. Hoare & Co – banks that, in the past, have looked after the financial affairs of the famous, and the infamous, ranging from Pitt the Younger and Oliver Cromwell to Lord Byron and Nell Gwynne.

They normally deal only with people whose income, or assets, are above minimum levels. Some, such as Child, Hoare and Adams & Co, consider each individual case on its merits.

But Coutts, for instance, demands that all applicants have an annual income above £100,000, or free assets worth at least £150,000. Nor is there any point in applying to Barclays Private Bank unless you have assets worth at least £250,000. Midland's and Lloyds' private banking operations set lower levels – of £75,000 and £100,000 respectively.

Wealth limits are not necessarily the only requirement. Some will only accept individuals of 'the right sort', thus ruling out the vulgar Pop Larkins of the world. Hoares, for instance, expects new customers to be introduced by existing clients. Quite often it would also expect a professional recommendation by a solicitor or accountant. Others will interview a much wider selection of potential clients. It is, in any case, unusual to be accepted by any private bank without a face-to-face interview. Private banking operations run by the high-street banks tend to pick up most of their customers from the main branch network. Lloyds and Midland allow people to keep their existing accounts at the old branches, and allocate private banking staff to look after their affairs. National Westminster, which owns Coutts, takes a more traditional approach, however. Those wishing to switch to Coutts are interviewed about their background and financial affairs and, if accepted, their accounts are then transferred to the new bank.

Fees can be a matter of negotiation. Most private banks prefer to offer full discretionary advice and charge a percentage of the value of the portfolio. Average fees range from 0.75 per cent to 1.5 per cent of value, normally subject to a minimum charge. Banking services tend to be free, often subject to a minimum balance, although neither Lloyds nor Midland imposes a lower limit.

PRIVATISATION

Selling off the family silver, as the late Harold MacMillan once described privatisation, turned Britain into a nation of

PRIVATISATION STOCKS

Company	Date	Price at issue date (p)	Price 29/10/95 (p)	% change	Total return*	Dividend index †
British Petroleum	Oct 87	265	465.5	76	11784	966
Cable & Wireless	Nov 81	28	423	1410	2112	823
Amersham International	Feb 82	142	948	580	1003	443
Associated British Ports	Feb 83	14	304	2079	3291	518
Enterprise Oil	Jun 84	172	339	95	332	215
British Telecom	Nov 84	130	370	185	496	454
TSB Group	Oct 86	100	373	273	600	212
British Gas	Dec 86	135	233	73	311	363
British Airways	Feb 87	120	470	292	588	314
Rolls-Royce	May 87	165	150	-10	142	98
BAA	Jul 87	122.5	496	302	524	279
British Steel	Dec 88	125	153	22	196	100
Anglian Water	Dec 89	240	565	135	337	170
North West Water	Dec 89	240	575	140	359	163
Northumbrian Water Group	Dec 89	240	1003	318	581	152
Severn Trent	Dec 89	240	623	160	391	153
South-West Water	Dec 89	240	501	109	314	147
Southern Water	Dec 89	240	665	177	409	173
Thames Water	Dec 89	240	524	118	315	167
Welsh Water	Dec 89	250	744	198	436	203
Wessex Water	Dec 89	120	317	164	388	178
Yorkshire Water	Dec 89	240	606	153	362	179
East Midlands Electricity	Dec 90	270	897	232	482	170
Eastern Group	Dec 90	240	976	307	529	196
London Electricity	Dec 90	240	907	278	488	195
ManWeb	Dec 90	240	1000	317	539	186
Midlands Electricity	Dec 90	240	969	304	520	198
Northern Electricity	Dec 90	215	875	307	614	203
NorWeb	Dec 90	240	1191	396	617	147
Seeboard	Dec 90	120	531	343	555	196
South Wales Electricity	Dec 90	240	926	286	491	181
South Western Electricity	Dec 90	240	900	275	484	191
Southern Electricity	Dec 90	240	955	298	513	197
Yorkshire Electricity	Dec 90	272	898	230	486	173
National Power	Mar 91	175	484	177	347	187
PowerGen	Mar 91	175	560	220	395	180
Scottish Hydro-Electric	Jun 91	240	337	40	171	138
Scottish Power	Jun 91	240	350	45	175	135
Northern Ireland Electricity	Jun 93	220	442	101	231	71

* The total return shows income plus capital growth as an index number, the base being 100 on the day a company's shares were floated.

† The dividend index shows the growth of dividends per share net of tax, with first dividend date being 100

Note: All prices are fully adjusted for capital changes.

For British Petroleum data is taken from 1987 privatisation issue for prices and from 30/12/64 for returns.

Source: Datastream

fortune-hunting stock market speculators. But the money-making story of the 1980s and early 1990s has turned sour. The process of reversing the postwar trend of nationalisation has resulted in a cacophony of protest aimed at the people who run the businesses, centring on sleaze, greed and inefficiency.

It is over a decade since British Telecom became a publicly quoted company with shareholders after a stock market flotation. The government's ownership of BT has been disposed of in three tranches, starting in 1984, with the second in December 1991 and the last one in July 1993. BT was the grandfather of privatisation. It epitomised all that was good about the Thatcher dream of turning inefficient state-owned companies into streamlined, efficient, profit-making private enterprises while creating a 'share-owning democracy'.

But opinion polls now paint a very different picture. Only one-sixth of voters favour water privatisation, just one-quarter back gas and electricity privatisation, while a staggering two-thirds favour renationalisation of both the water and power industries. Even British Telecom, the jewel in the privatisation crown, would be better off back in state hands, according to nearly half of all voters. Why such a violent reaction against privatisation? Surely the process has made a lot of money for a lot of people? In fact the table opposite shows just how much money some people were able to make.

Well, there are several reasons for this reaction:

● First of all, the intellectual arguments of the early 1980s are returning. The fundamental question asked by opponents of privatisation is: how can the government sell a nationalised industry back to the taxpayers who already own and pay for it?
● The privatisation of the water companies and the electricity companies (the utilities) has given rise to claims of greed. People argue that the directors of privatised companies have enjoyed huge windfall gains from massive salary rises and executive share option schemes at the expense of

both shareholders and customers, most noticeably Cedric Brown of British Gas who was awarded a 75 per cent pay rise in November 1994.

- The handling of the sale of some of the public companies has also proved controversial, leading to allegations of sleaze and insider dealing. The March 1995 sale of the two power generating firms, PowerGen and National Power, led to accusations that the government had misled more than a million people by failing to disclose a new round of price capping planned by the electricity regulator, which was eventually announced two days after the £4bn flotation. Investors' paper profits were almost wiped out in two days of furious selling. In June the Treasury launched an internal enquiry into the sell-off after a leaked letter revealed that the Stock Exchange had been investigating allegations of insider dealing.

- The long hot summer of 1995 brought claims of incompetence from customers who had to suffer hosepipe bans and rationing in some areas such as North Yorkshire as the recently privatised water companies battled to stop precious water reserves leaking away through damaged mains.

Future privatisations such as British Rail and British Nuclear Fuels, as well as the private building and running of prisons, therefore face stiff opposition from voters and politicians. Labour has already committed itself to keeping the railways in public ownership.

Privatisation has become one of Britain's biggest exports, with European governments copying the British example with plans for privatisations worth £130bn over the next five years. A whole new industry has sprung up around privatisations. Share Shops have become a feature of our high streets where ordinary people can go to buy shares easily and conveniently without having to go through the often intimidating process of using a stockbroker. Through privatisations people have become familiar with such stock-market beasts as **stags**. These are investors who buy into a new issue of shares through a flotation and then sell a few days later once the share price has risen.

Privatisation has also given gainful employment for the country's ever-growing legion of regulators. Each privatised industry, such as gas or electricity, has a regulator. One of their most important roles is to control prices. They do this by setting the amount by which the privatised industries are allowed to increase prices each year. Normally this is set at a figure equal to the rate of inflation minus X. This price formula is reviewed every five years and is supposed to result in the privatised companies becoming more efficient. In theory, if the companies know by how much the prices they charge will be increased each year they can increase profits by cutting costs.

Q is for:

QUOTED COMPANY

This is the colloquial term most people use to describe companies that have sold shares in their businesses to the public by obtaining a listing on a stock market. In Britain most companies that go public join the **Official List** run by the **London Stock Exchange**. It is possible to become a quoted company and obtain a listing on other exchanges such as the **Alternative Investment Market (AIM)** or **Tradepoint**, but the London Stock Exchange is still by far the most important market for shares in the UK. So why do companies go public and how do they do it?

There are more than 2,000 quoted or listed companies on the London Stock Exchange. There are four main reasons why a company in private ownership might want to go public or **float**. These are as follows:

1. prestige;
2. growth;
3. access to capital; and
4. visibility, or publicity.

With these advantages come three main obligations for a public company, which are:

Companies often see joining the Stock Exchange's Official List as a boost to their prestige

1. accountability;
2. responsibility; and
3. regulation.

Public companies and their directors have to comply with an enormous amount of regulation. The rules exist primarily to ensure that a fair, equitable and efficient market is maintained at all times in the market for shares for all participants, be they investors or the companies themselves.

The Stock Exchange enforces the rules that relate to a company obtaining a quote on the Official List. The listing rules are commonly known as the **Yellow Book**. Then there is the **Companies Act 1985** (amended in 1989), which lays down the law on disclosure of interest in shares. This enables public companies and their shareholders to identify significant shareholdings. The Act also sets out the rules for company investigations. Under **Section 212** a public company is allowed to find out who its shareholders are at any point in time. This might sound strange as public companies are obliged to keep a **register** of shareholder's names, but these registers are often a few weeks out of date, which, during a hostile takeover bid, can be significant. Shareholdings may also be held through a **nominee** company. A Section 212 investigation forces a nominee to reveal who the real shareholder is.

The Companies Act also governs the statutory requirements for company meetings such as the **annual general meeting (AGM)**, and also the documentation that a company must keep, the most important ones being its **memorandum and articles of association**.

If that was not enough, public companies have to observe the rulings and code of conduct published by the **Panel on Takeovers and Mergers (POTAM)**, rules governing substantial acquisition of shares – otherwise known as **dawn or market raids** – and the rules of the **Monopolies and Mergers Commission**.

But to return to the Stock Exchange and going public, companies often see joining the Official List as a boost to *prestige*. A quoted company may enhance its standing within the financial community and enjoy greater confidence in its business by being listed.

Another important reason for going public is to fund future *growth* and investment. The initial listing or **flotation** can be used to issue more shares in a company. The investors who buy the shares provide extra capital for a company, which it can use to fund future growth. Later on, the Stock Exchange provides various means for companies to raise extra cash. Going public allows a company to use the capital raised from issuing new shares to pay off bank loans, a process known as **swapping debt for equity**, while borrowing money from the bank in future may be easier for a public company than a private one.

Access to capital is perhaps the main reason why a company uses a Stock Exchange to go public. The Stock Exchange fulfils a dual function. Raising capital for companies and then providing a means for investors to sell their shareholdings for cash if they wish to get out. The capital raising function is called the **primary market,** and the share trading function, the **secondary market.**

A useful spin-off from going public is *publicity*, although this can backfire, of course. Quoted companies are under intense scrutiny as investors demand to know everything there is to know about a company before committing their money. When a company first comes to the stock market it is big news in the financial pages of national newspapers and magazines. These publications tend to concentrate their coverage on public companies and the things they produce, rather than on private companies.

The Stock Exchange is responsible for screening applications to the Official List. It monitors companies' ongoing compliance with the rules and is responsible for dealing with any rule breaches. It also regulates the secondary market, and must ensure that dealing in shares takes place in an orderly and efficient trading manner.

To win a place on the Official List company directors must prepare a **prospectus**. This provides investors with a complete picture of the company, including its trading history, financial record, management and business prospects.

The Yellow Book sets out certain basic conditions that a company wishing to go public must meet, which are as follows:

- Expected market value of shares must be at least £700,000 or £200,000 for bonds.
- Shares must be freely transferable.
- The company should have a three-year trading record.
- At least 25 per cent of any class of shares is to be in the hands of the public.

- Listing particulars and prospectuses must be lodged at least 48 hours before hearing of the application by the **Committee on Quotations,** a Stock Exchange body.
- A company will not be admitted to the Official List if it has a single corporate shareholder holding 30 per cent or more of shares where there is a conflict of interest with other shareholders.
- Shareholders of quoted companies must be given **pre-emptive rights.** This means any share issue made for cash must be offered to existing shareholders in proportion to their holdings. The UK is virtually alone in having this rule, which is designed to stop people's shareholdings being diluted.
- All quoted companies must agree to comply with the Yellow Book's **continuing obligations.** These include notifying the Stock Exchange of price-sensitive information, notifying it of dividends, and issuing half-yearly reports within four months and annual accounts within six months of the year end.

There are three methods for companies to go public and become a quoted company. The most appropriate method depends on cost and whether or not new money is to be raised. The three methods are:

1. **Offer for sale** This allows a company to invite subscriptions from both institutional and private investors. The shares available may be new ones being sold for cash or existing ones held by current shareholders. The offer for sale is organised by a company's **sponsor,** normally a firm of stockbrokers. It will also be **underwritten.** This means that for a fee a sponsor will buy any shares left over after the offer for sale closes in order to make sure that a company's aims are achieved. To spread the risk a main underwriter may persuade other institutions to underwrite part of an offer. Application forms and prospectuses should be advertised in the national press and be available

through outlets such as high-street banks. The offer normally takes place at a fixed price per share.

2. **Placing** The most common method for going public for
   smaller companies, a placing is a low-cost, low-key affair,
   with no widespread advertising and less publicity. A placing allows a company's sponsor or stockbroker to offer
   new or existing shares selectively to its own client base, be
   they institutions or private clients.
3. **Introduction** Shares can be introduced to the Official List
   by companies that already have widely held share capital
   with 25 per cent already in the public's hands. In an
   introduction no money is raised and no new shares are
   issued. As a result there are no underwriting costs and only
   small advertising requirements. An introduction is the
   least expensive way of flotation.

Already quoted companies can issue new shares to existing
shareholders to raise extra cash through a **rights issue**,
explained in more detail on pages 205–6. Rights issues must
observe investors' pre-emptive rights.

Shareholders will expect quoted companies to pay a **dividend**, normally paid in two amounts: an interim dividend, and
a final dividend six months later. Dividends are paid on **ordinary shares**, the main form of capital issued by quoted companies. To raise capital they can also issue **bonds**, which pay
investors a fixed amount of interest each year. Some arrange
for **options** and **warrants** to be issued, linked to their ordinary
shares. Other types of capital issues include convertibles,
preference shares and convertible preference shares.

$\mathcal{R}$ is for:

RATIOS

Number crunching is big business in the City of London. Stockbrokers and fund managers employ an army of **analysts** to peer into the maze of facts and figures published by quoted companies to decide whether shares should be bought, sold or held. The basic ingredients of an analyst's statistical diet are **investment ratios**. By calculating these and comparing one company's ratios with another, analysts come up with opinions about companies that stockbrokers use to persuade clients to trade shares (which earns them commission). A company's vital statistics are the following:

- **Earnings per share (eps)** Calculated by dividing the profit attributable to shareholders by the number of shares in issue. This is the **basic eps**. Some companies have a **fully diluted eps**. This takes account of new shares that may be issued when **warrants** or **convertibles** are exercised. As a result, the fully diluted eps may be lower than the basic eps.
- **Price-earnings ratio (P/E)** This ratio uses the eps to express the number of years' earnings the stock market expects from a company, based on the current share price. It is calculated by dividing the current share price by the eps. So, if a company's earnings (as detailed in its report

Stockbrokers and fund managers employ an army of analysts to peer into the maze of facts and figures published by quoted companies

and accounts) were £40m, with 250 million shares in issue at 300p per share, the P/E ratio would be 18.7, also expressed as **18.7 times earnings**. The P/E is perhaps the most commonly quoted ratio. It is only useful when compared to the P/E ratios of other companies in the same business. If an industry's average P/E is ten but one company has a P/E of 15, that would suggest its shares are in big demand because above average earnings growth is expected. If a P/E is below average, this indicates a company out of favour and with poor growth prospects.

- **Dividend yield**   Calculated by dividing the gross dividend per share by the current market price per share. Companies with relatively high dividend yields are those out of favour or considered risky. A low share price will tend to give higher dividend yields. Thus companies with low P/E ratios tend to have high dividend yields and vice versa.

- **Dividend cover** This shows the likelihood of an existing dividend being maintained in the future by a company. It is calculated by dividing the eps by the net dividend per share. Companies with an above-average dividend cover could be criticised for being mean with its dividends, although it could argue it was simply being prudent.
- **Net asset value** Calculated by dividing a company's net assets by the number of shares in issue. A share price may be above or below the net asset value per share figure. This reflects investors' views as to the ability of a company to generate growth on its assets. It is of particular relevance to investment trust and property companies.

RECESSION

A word that British families are all too familiar with. Recessions have a permanent place in history. The last one we faced lasted from October 1990 well into the spring of 1993. For once it was not a recession based mainly in the traditional manufacturing and industrial areas of the North and the Midlands (blighted by the previous recession of the early 1980s), but one that hit the South East, with its predominance of service industries, just as hard.

Even now the recovery is fragile, always seemingly on the verge of falling back into a downturn. But why do recessions happen and what can be done to stop them?

In the first two years of the last recession Britain's **gross national product** fell 4 per cent. We inherited from the 1980s a huge mountain of debt run up by both households and companies. As we entered the nervous 1990s one thing the economy needed was low interest rates to stop this debt burden proving too expensive to repay. If it became too costly, people and companies would be forced into bankruptcy. Instead, however, the policy on interest rates, known as **monetary policy,** was to increase the cost of borrowing. This was because the 1980s debt mountain was not a root cause of recession, rather a symptom of that decade's fast and furious growth rates. Taxes had been cut to fuel an unprecedented consumer boom. The late 1980s saw **inflation** taking off as the economy over-heated.

The big difference going into the 1990s was the UK's membership of the European **Exchange Rate Mechanism (ERM)**. This effectively took control of domestic monetary policy away from the government. The chancellor's hands were tied. The ERM required Britain to link the value of the pound to that of the Deutschmark. This was part of the long and still troubled road European economies are supposed to be travelling to **economic union** and a **single currency**.

The theory was that by linking the value of the two currencies the British economy would converge with that of Germany's, producing similar rates of growth, inflation, interest rates and employment. But at that time the Bundesbank needed high interest rates in Germany to control the inflation caused by the unification of East and West Germany. High interest rates made the German currency attractive to investors, which bid up the value of the Deutschmark. To keep the pound within sight of the Deutschmark the chancellor, Norman Lamont, had to keep increasing UK interest rates. The higher UK interest rates went, the more attractive buying pounds became to the big institutional investors, who buy and sell currencies to get the best returns available.

The gridlock of the ERM thus fuelled recessionary problems back home. Interest rates had to be kept high to keep the pound in line with the Deutschmark, and so the debt burden from the 1980s became costlier and costlier. Companies defaulted and the banks closed them down. Consumers could not afford to spend as they battled to pay off debt, which meant they certainly could not afford to borrow money to spend.

The biggest part of consumer debt was in the form of mortgages, most of which were variable rate loans that rose with base rates. These became too costly, ending in a wave of repossessions across the UK. Confidence in the housing market collapsed, as did prices, in a downward spiral of misery. If house prices fall UK consumer confidence falls, yet another dent to any potential recovery.

Another consequence of linking the pound to the Deutschmark was to make British exports very expensive and uncompetitive. But, at the same time, imports became relatively cheaper. A large **trade deficit** (the difference between our exports and imports) arose, a situation that was almost unheard of during previous recessions. As more and more people were laid off, so government spending increased on unemployment benefits and other social security measures. Thus the government was spending far more than it was earning from its dwindling tax revenues, resulting in a big **public sector borrowing requirement (PSBR)** and plunging the government deeper and deeper into debt.

When a recession results in **twin deficits** (the trade deficit and the PSBR), the situation is grave indeed. Something had to give. The action returned to the foreign exchange markets. Speculators could see that the economic situation in Britain was untenable. They believed that the government's nerve would crack as domestic political survival became more important than economic union with the rest of Europe. As a result, players like the **hedge fund** manager **George Soros** made huge multibillion dollar bets that the pound would fall in value. They started selling pounds faster than the Bank of England could buy them.

To mop up this supply and to try and stop the value of the pound falling, the chancellor had two basic tactics he could pursue. One was to **talk up** the pound. This involves the chancellor in Parliament or standing outside his 11 Downing Street residence, insisting that the government is committed to its monetary policy to drive down inflation and achieve sustainable growth. This is supposed to send a message to the markets that interest rates are not going to fall. The second tactic is to take more direct action and actually increase the level of interest rates. Clearly the former is less expensive if it works.

The problem in 1991 was that no one believed the chancellor's attempts to talk up the pound, so he increased interest rates – until Wednesday 16 September 1992 when UK base rates went up to an economically crippling 15 per cent. The ERM cracked and out fell the pound. The government decided to suspend our membership of the ERM, which meant the pound was free to float on the foreign exchange markets and find its own level (**equilibrium**). As a consequence, UK interest rates could be cut. Down they came, germinating the first seeds of recovery.

The speculators, such as Soros, who forced the pound out of the ERM, also profited. Having sold their expensive pounds before 21 September they were able to buy them back far more cheaply once the pound had left the ERM, pocketing the difference, which in Soros's case was $1bn.

The Conservatives say they have learnt from the mistakes of their giveaway budgets of the 1980s that caused the economy to overheat. They now want to follow the traditional German model of low inflation and sustainable growth. They believe that following this course will allow us to arrive at a situation where the economy could fit easily with those of a European economic union.

Nevertheless, such a situation will take a long time for British workers and consumers to adjust to. Property can no longer be expected to be the long-term store of wealth it once was. This realisation has already curbed consumer confidence, proving the point that the **feelgood factor** is just a polite expression for house price inflation. Low inflation has driven down costs and wages, making the UK far more competitive, especially compared to the rest of Europe, but a prerequisite for this competitiveness is a more flexible labour market, which in layman's terms means a much less secure labour market. Jobs offer much less permanency and security, again reducing the incentive to spend.

We are now in a period of adjustment, a period in which we

could leave the old **boom-bust cycle** behind *if* we are willing to live with the more austere consequences of low inflation and low interest rates.

REDUNDANCY

Losing your job is normally rated as only slightly less stressful than bereavement, or getting divorced. In some ways, the effects are similar. For instance, as with losing a spouse, unemployment deprives people of a perceived social identity and takes away an important central prop to their lives.

People who are made redundant qualify for a statutory minimum payment if they have worked at least 16 hours a week for the same employer for more than two years, or at least eight hours for more than five. The minimum payment is not generous – 1–1½ week's pay, up to £210, for each completed year. However, many employers choose to pay more. You do not have to pay tax on redundancy payments below £30,000. Payments above this amount are normally taxed at your highest marginal rate. All redundancy payments must be declared in tax returns.

In recent years, the Inland Revenue has tended to interpret more strictly the rules governing redundancy payments. For instance, you may now have problems in taking the full amount tax-free if your contract mentioned specific dismissal terms. Generous severance agreements that, for example, preclude working for a competitor for a specific length of time, or contain promises not to sue for unfair dismissal, may also cause problems with the taxman. On the other hand, you may be entitled to more generous tax relief if your period of employment included time spent overseas, or you are leaving because of ill-health.

If you have lost your job because the company has gone bust, the Department of Trade and Industry assumes responsibility for redundancy payments, plus any salary arrears and holiday pay. If your contract entitles you to payments above your minimum statutory rights, you will have to join the list of preferential creditors.

Some companies offer enhanced pension rights in lieu of redundancy payments. These may be worth considering, especially for people who are in line for very large pay-offs.

REGULATORY AUTHORITIES

It seems difficult to move these days without bumping into some kind of regulator. They are everywhere. The telephone you ring, the gas you burn, the electricity you switch on, the water you drink are all provided under the watchful gaze of a regulatory body. Oftel, Ofgas, Offer, Ofwat are the now familiar names of the utility regulators that have sprung up since privatisation. Their role is to maintain a competitive marketplace for the various commodities under their jurisdiction and to ensure that consumers are protected from unfair pricing and other monopolistic activity.

But the granddaddy of all regulation is the **Financial Services Act 1986**, which spawned the regulatory authorities that now police the financial services industry (life assurance, pensions and investments). This Act gives the Chancellor of the Exchequer statutory powers to regulate financial services for the protection of consumers.

It was the collapse of a small investment firm called **Norton Warburg** in the early 1980s that spurred Margaret Thatcher's government into action. Norton Warburg went down taking £8m of clients' money with it. In a decade that was supposed to be rediscovering the concept of self-help and embracing the notion of a share-owning democracy it was not acceptable to have the investment industry crawling with crooks and spivs. It was time to get rid of them.

Thus **Professor Laurence Gower** chaired a committee which somewhat inevitably concluded that the best way forward was to introduce an Act of Parliament, which took effect from 1988. It provides for a hierarchy of power. The

Treasury can delegate its powers under the Act to a **designated agency**, which in this case is the **Securities and Investments Board (SIB)**. This body in turn delegates certain powers for regulating specific parts of the industry to **self-regulatory bodies (SROs)**. As the name suggests, these allow representatives of the insurance and investment companies to have a big say in the detailed rules and regulations that control their day-to-day activity, be it sales, marketing, administration or fund management.

There are now three SROs. Anyone who wants to conduct investment business has to be a member of one of the following:

1. The **Personal Investment Authority (PIA)** The SRO responsible for the sales and marketing activities of companies providing life assurance, pensions and investments such as unit trusts. Companies or individuals offering independent financial advice also have to be members of the PIA and comply with its rules.
2. **Investment Management Regulatory Organisation (Imro)** The body which monitors companies undertaking fund management. It was this SRO that took the rap for the Maxwell pensions scandal.
3. The **Securities and Futures Authority (SFA)** The SRO which controls the activities of stockbrokers who buy and sell shares, bonds and derivatives for clients.

Some companies are authorised to undertake investment business through membership of a **recognised professional body (RPB)**. Organisations such as the **Law Society** and the **Institute of Chartered Accountants** qualify as RPBs and are considered to control their member firms (solicitors and accountants respectively) to a high degree.

There has been much criticism of the Financial Services Act and the number of rules and regulations it lays down. The cost of regulating just the retail end of financial services, mainly through the PIA, is running at £330m a year. There are some signs that the chief regulator, the SIB, believes that the industry has cleaned itself up sufficiently to allow some relaxation of the rules.

Any person or company discovered conducting unauthorised investment business faces the following penalties:

- A maximum six months in gaol and a maximum £5,000 fine if prosecuted through a magistrates' court.
- A maximum two years in gaol and an unlimited fine if prosecuted in a Crown Court.

RETAIL PRICES INDEX (RPI)

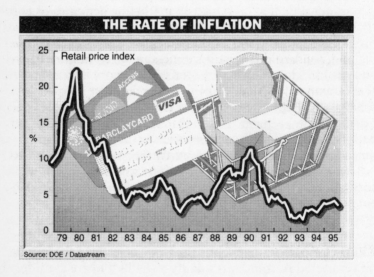

THE RATE OF INFLATION

Source: DOE / Datastream

The RPI is a measure used to track the buying power of the money in our pockets. It is often referred to as the **cost-of-living index,** or **inflation,** although purists would argue that neither description is strictly accurate. There are two types: **headline** inflation, which includes changes in mortgage interest payments, and **underlying** inflation, which does not.

The original cost-of-living index, which began in 1914, was very much more limited in its application than its modern equivalent. It covered basic consumer commodities, such as bread, potatoes, clothing materials, lamp oil and candles, but not, for instance, fresh fruit, biscuits and cakes, or electricity. Nowadays, it is intended to reflect the cost of practically everything on which the ordinary consumer spends his or her money, including travel and entertainment. However, certain services are excluded because, according to the Central Statistical Office, they are too difficult to assess. These include life assurance, betting, cash gifts, income tax and National Insurance contributions.

The RPI is compiled from about 130,000 separate price quotations collected each month, mainly by personal visits to shops all over the country. These are then divided into five broad groups: food and catering, alcohol and tobacco, housing and household expenditure, personal expenditure, travel and leisure. The index is weighted to give more importance to some components than to others. For instance, a given percentage rise in the price of bread has about four times the effect on the index as a similar increase in the price of butter. That is because the average household spends roughly four times as much on bread than it does on butter.

The whole operation is overseen by an independent advisory committee, whose members include consumers, retailers, employers and employees.

RIGHTS ISSUE

This is how a quoted company raises new capital by issuing new shares after its initial **flotation** on a stock market such as the London Stock Exchange. Rights issues must be made to present shareholders in proportion to their existing shareholdings – this rule is known as **pre-emptive rights**.

The capital raised from a rights issue is used for a variety of purposes, such as funding an acquisition, paying for new factories, or paying off debts. To persuade shareholders to subscribe to a rights issue the new shares will be offered at a discount to the market price.

A company might have five million 20p shares in issue at a market price of 100p. It decides to make a rights issue of one new share for every four held at 75p a share. An investor who owns four shares has an investment worth £4 (4 × 100p). If that investor takes up his or her rights, he or she will end up with four shares worth £4 and one share worth 75p, making a total of five shares costing £4.75 or 95p a share, known as the **ex-rights price**. However, the investor does not have to subscribe to a rights issue. He or she can sell his or her rights to subscribe, and would then receive the ex-rights price minus the subscription price, i.e. 95p − 75p = 20p. This is the **nil paid price**.

Alternatively, investors can **split their rights**. This allows investors without enough cash to subscribe for their full rights to buy some of their rights. If an investor had 4,000 shares in the above company he or she would be offered 1,000 new shares under the one-for-four rights issue. The number of shares an investor could subscribe for by splitting his or her rights in the above example would be calculated by dividing the nil paid price by the ex rights price multiplied by the number of shares on offer under the rights issue. Thus 20p ÷ 95p × 1,000 = £210.52. This calculation can be checked by multiplying £210.52 by the 75p subscription price which equals £157.89. This money will be found by selling the remaining 789.48 shares at the nil paid price of 20p which raises £157.90.

ROLLING SETTLEMENT

For many years settling up with a stockbroker after buying or selling shares was a complicated affair. Things have now been simplified and since July of this year people have had five working days to pay for shares they have bought or to supply shares they have sold under the system of rolling settlement.

Before this system was introduced people had anything from a few days to three weeks to settle up under the arcane and antiquated system of **account settlement**. This was because the Stock Exchange nominated certain dates during the year when everyone would settle their accounts, be they buying or selling. These accounts were between two and three weeks apart, depending on whether there was a bank holiday or other interruption to the calendar. Investors could buy and sell within an account period without spending any cash and still make a profit if share prices went up. Or people could sell shares they did not own and buy them back later on in the account period. If share prices had fallen they could pocket the difference between the price they got for selling and the price they had to pay to buy the shares. This type of business was called **intra-account trading**.

However, rolling settlement now means that every day is a settlement day instead of specific days in the calendar. Thus everyone must pay for shares five days after buying them or supply shares five days after selling them. The UK is moving to three-day rolling settlement, bringing it into line with other major stock markets such as New York.

ROYAL MINT

The Royal Mint is responsible for producing the ordinary coins in our pockets, a job it has been doing in one guise or another since **Alfred the Great** invaded London in AD 886. In the twelfth century minting was concentrated in the **Tower of London** at a time when minting could be a dangerous occupation. King **Henry I** had the hands of 96 coin makers or **moneyers** cut off for producing substandard coins. At this time the Mint came under the control of a master moneyer. The present master is the Chancellor of the Exchequer although the day-to-day running of the operation is the responsibility of the deputy master and chief executive appointed by the Treasury.

The history of the Royal Mint is closely tied to the political history of the nation. The first coins of the republican commonwealth in the seventeenth century are alone in using completely English inscriptions. They were inscribed with *Commonwealth of England* on one side and *God is with Us* on the other. All other coins have used Latin inscriptions. Indeed what appears on coins has always been a sensitive subject. **Edward VIII** insisted that the Mint should break with its tradition of alternating the profile of the monarch with each succession. His father George V had faced left on coins. Edward VIII's vanity caused him to insist on also facing left – what he considered his better side – instead of right.

The Royal Mint was moved out of the Tower in 1811 to take advantage of new steam-driven technology that was considered too dangerous to house in the same building as a large arsenal. It moved across the road to Tower Hill where it remained until 1971 and **decimalisation**. At this point the old plant was unable to cope with the requirements of producing a completely new range of coins, and a new site was therefore opened at Llantrisant in South Wales. Making coins, both for ourselves and for overseas markets, has now become a profitable business for the modern Royal Mint. In the 1994–95 financial year the Royal Mint made a profit of £15m on total sales of £106.5m. Of these sales £70.3m were made to 74 overseas countries, from Armenia to Zimbabwe and Croatia to Thailand. In the same year, total issues of UK circulating coins were 7.4 per cent higher than 1993–94, at 1.4 billion coins, thanks to heavy demand for 1p and 2p coins. One thing the Royal Mint does not make are bank notes which is the responsibility of the Bank of England.

S *is for:*

SCHOOL FEES

A recent Gallup survey for insurer Eagle Star found that nearly one in five British parents want to send their children to private school and a glance at the Department of Education's performance tables explains why. At both 'A' Level and GCSE, independent schools head the lists. But closer examination shows there are plenty of state schools – comprehensives, grammar schools, sixth form colleges, and colleges of further education – that offer top value for money, with high levels of attainment available for free. Clearly an excellent education can be had from the state, but the problem is access to these top state schools. Also the gap between the good schools and the bad schools is widening, fuelling parents' fears that their children may be left behind simply because their Local Education Authority is below the national average.

So, having decided that little Johnny or Jenny must go to an independent school, and having scoured the league tables for the best performers in your general area, how do you go about paying for a school fees bill that will cost an average of £50,000 at one of the country's senior day schools over seven years, assuming fees rise by a conservative 5 per cent each year? The options are as follows:

Fees at one of the country's senior day schools will total an average of £50,000 over seven years

- Pay out of **existing savings or income,** which is probably an option only for the lucky few. Some families will have grandparents willing to pay a lump sum or regular payments to meet school fees.
- Some form of school fees planning will be necessary for most. Start as early as possible and choose the most **flexible** and **tax efficient** available. Do not be bamboozled by cleverly packaged school fee plans from insurers or unit trust companies. These can be expensive and difficult to get your money out if you have a change of heart about private schooling. It will be cheaper and more flexible to save for school fees through your own choice of **Tessa, deposit account, National Savings,** or **unit and investment trusts** wrapped inside the tax-free shelter of a **Personal Equity Plan (Pep).** These forms of school fees saving particularly suit those who start early.
- A common plan sold by insurers is a package of **endowment policies** with maturity payouts designed to coincide

with annual school bills. Regular premiums to pay for the policies are funded out of parents' income. Returns are only average but involve little risk. Maturity payments when they arrive can be spent on other things if private schooling is no longer a priority, but early encashment will result in poor surrender values.

- **Composition schemes,** which are run by the schools themselves. Parents pay a lump sum before their children start. This is invested by the school and is then used to pay bills as they arise. If the lump sum is paid over early and invested well, parents can make big savings over the years. Parents should check what rate of return a school needs to earn to pay fees and where the money is invested. Parents may also be penalised if a child does not attend the school chosen or leaves early.

- **Educational trusts** are more flexible than composition schemes. They buy annuities to fund school fees but can switch payment from one school to another, and will normally guarantee to repay money should the cash no longer be required for school fees. Another version is the **back-to-back** scheme that involves using a lump sum to buy an annuity, which is then used to pay for a series of insurance policies. These meet school fees when they fall due.

SHARES

These are issued by companies who want to raise capital from investors to expand or improve their businesses. In return, investors expect to share in a company's profits. They do this by receiving regular **dividends** from the company, usually twice a year in the form of an **interim** and a **final dividend.** Any company can issue shares, be it a **private** company or a **public** company with shares listed on a stock market. Mostly people read or hear about shares issued by public companies, as they are the most widely available and the most widely held.

Ordinary shares issued by the best companies are called **blue chips**. Those issued by the very small quoted companies that generate little interest and are generally below 50p are called **penny shares**.

The most common type of share is the **ordinary share**. Holders of these are entitled to a dividend and also to a **vote** at company meetings. Although directors run a company, the shareholders own it. Ordinary shares can carry the most risk, but also the biggest potential return. Some companies have more complicated share structures than simply issuing ordinary shares. They issue different types of shares and bestow different voting rights on different classes of shareholder. Ordinary shares make up most of a company's **equity capital**. This is capital that is entitled to a variable and hopefully growing dividend. **Participating preference shares** are also classed as equity capital. Most preference shares have a fixed dividend that must be paid before other shareholders, while participating preference shares can receive a dividend above the fixed payout.

Share prices are closely monitored by investors and stockmarket commentators. A share price is determined by the supply and demand for it in the market. If demand is strong a price will rise. Demand, though, is based on investors' perception of a company's fortunes, and if the future looks bad, investors will turn sellers and the supply of the shares on the stock market will increase, thus forcing the price down.

Some share prices languish simply because the companies that issued them are not well understood by investors, and few people notice them even though their businesses may be doing well. These shares are said to be undervalued. A perceptive investor can buy these undervalued shares and make a killing once the rest of the market catches up. And catch up it should, because the stock market is supposed to be an efficient market where all the buyers and sellers have the same access at the same time to all the information available. However, this tends to encourage the **herd** instinct, which still produces at least temporary inefficiencies that astute investors can profit from before the crowd realises and stampedes in.

SHARE EXCHANGE SCHEMES

Although fans of privatisation are proud of spreading wider share ownership, the truth is that many individual investors own only a handful of shares. This is particularly true about the privatisation issues, which were heavily oversubscribed, leaving lots of people with very small shareholdings. Often these people would be better off investing in a more diversified and less risky portfolio offered by a unit trust or an investment trust. But the cost of selling the shares and reinvesting them can be prohibitive.

This is where the share exchange scheme comes in. Fund management companies running investment trusts or unit trusts will offer to buy these small parcels of shares cheaply and reinvest the proceeds in one of their own funds. Sometimes the companies will waive the charges altogether.

But people must be happy with the trust they are being offered. Share exchange schemes should not be seen purely as an easy, low-cost way of offloading a small shareholding. You will be buying into another investment and you must satisfy yourself that you really want it. Quite often a fund manager will promote a share exchange scheme linked to a trust that has not been performing very well as a way of generating some extra demand for it. Moreover the fund management companies offering the schemes can be quite fussy about which company's shares they will accept, often specifying that only certain shares qualify for the exchange. If a shareholding is below a minimum size they may expect you to top up the shareholding with cash.

There are several unit trust companies who are willing to exchange any Stock Exchange quoted shares and bonds, including gilts, as well as units in other fund managers' trusts.

SHARE OPTIONS

Share options are not just for executive fat cats. The Inland
Revenue says 1.4 million people benefit from work-related
savings schemes that involve cheap shares or profit sharing.
The main ones are:

- **Savings-related share option schemes** People save between
  £5 and £250 a month into a designated deposit account for
  three years, after which they can take the cash or convert
  the proceeds into shares. By saving for three years people
  receive tax-free bonuses calculated by multiplying the
  monthly saving by nine, giving a tax-free return of 5.53 per
  cent. The price paid by people who decide to convert into
  shares is fixed at the start of the contract. These can be at
  discounts of as much as 20 per cent off the going market
  price. If the share price rises over the three years the
  compound returns can be much higher than those from
  deposit accounts. People who do not take shares can leave
  their cash on deposit for a further two years earning 5.87
  per cent tax-free.
- **Profit-sharing schemes** These schemes allow companies to
  give shares to workers employed for at least five years. A
  company sets up a trust and pays in money, normally a
  percentage of annual profits. The trustees use it to buy the
  company's shares on behalf of workers. Once granted,
  shares must be held for two years before being sold. If they
  are left with the trustees for three years they do not count
  as income. The value of shares granted in any tax year
  cannot exceed £3,000 or 10 per cent of a worker's annual
  earnings, whichever is greater.

  Shares worth up to £3,000 from both the above schemes
  can be transferred directly into a **single company Personal
  Equity Plan (Pep)** within 90 days to shelter future gains
  from income and capital gains tax.
- **Executive or discretionary share option schemes** The most
  controversial schemes, and it is under these schemes that

the bosses of the privatised utility companies have enjoyed huge windfall profits. In some cases they also transferred ownership of their shares to their wives, causing an outcry from MPs, but from a tax-planning view this was a very sensible move to take advantage of a spouse's £6,300 capital gains tax exemption.

The Revenue says that about 80,000 people are members of these schemes. The term 'executive' is misleading as any full-time worker can be granted options. The value of options is limited to £100,000 or four times current salary, whichever is greater. The option price can be set up to 15 per cent below the market price. Since the 1995 Budget, options granted where shares are worth £20,000 or less escape income tax. Options granted above this amount, and any increase in their value before the option is exercised, must be counted as income for tax purposes. Capital gains tax may be payable when the shares are sold, although employees do not have to exercise their options. Shares from this scheme must be **bed-and-breakfasted** before being placed in a Pep.

SHARE SHOPS

The idea of share shops was another privatisation spin-off. They were supposed to provide a high-street network of outlets which would allow any member of the public to walk in off the street and trade shares cheaply and quickly, in another measure to try and extend share ownership. Interest in share shops does become more prevalent at the time of a big privatisation issue, and such shops tend to be run by banks and building societies offering brokering services. But the interest among financial institutions is rarely sustained and the idea has never really caught the imagination of the public. Some big flotations other than privatisations, such as venture capital giant 3i, have used the idea of an organised distribution network to promote an offer, but they remain few and far between.

That said, the privatisation process has left behind it a number of stockbrokers, banks and building societies offering computer-based trading services in their branches that are the closest thing to the government's original share shop dream. There are several high-street stockbrokers who offer services that allow people to sell their shares within ten minutes and walk away with the proceeds. Buyers get contract notes on the spot and receive share certificates later. Some banks and building societies have stock-market screens in their branches where staff can explain the best buy and sell prices to customers and people can decide whether to trade. Investors do not have to be customers of the banks or building societies who offer these services but they may have to take a form of identification with them when they go to trade.

Probably a more popular way to buy shares these days is over the telephone, again on an instant dealing basis with trades executed while the customer is on the line.

STAMP DUTY

This is a tax levied on the transfer of shares and property and is paid by the purchaser. On shares the rate is 0.5 per cent but is always calculated in multiples of 50p per £100 or part thereof. So if someone buys £2,300 of shares the duty would be 0.5 times £2,300 which equals £11.50. Anything between £2,301 and £2,400 would be charged at 0.5 times £2,400 which equals £12. Charities are exempt from paying stamp duty. On property, people pay 1 per cent on any purchase of more than £60,000, so a house costing £72,000 would mean stamp duty payable of £720.

STATE EARNINGS-RELATED PENSIONS SCHEME
(Serps)

Started in 1978 by Labour minister Shirley Williams as an add-on to the basic state pension, it is paid for out of a worker's **National Insurance (NI)** contributions, with benefits based on the amount earned in a lifetime.

Since 1988 people have been allowed to **contract out** of Serps and have their relevant NI contributions paid into a **company pension scheme** or a **personal pension**. This opt out clause was designed to help the government reduce the state's pension bill and offer people the opportunity to turn their National Insurance contributions into a bigger pot by investing in a personal pension run by an insurer or fund management company. On retirement these people collect the basic state pension plus any income from their Serps rebate pension funds. As an incentive to encourage people out of Serps the government pays a sliding scale of incentives into the personal pension. Sadly if the Serps rebate pension fund performs badly people may not produce enough to make the move worthwhile. Older people who have contracted out may lose out because their rebate pensions may not have time enough to grow before they retire. Most experts have said that women aged 37 or more and men of 44 or over should not contract out. Those that have already done so are often advised to contract back in, unless they are willing to take an investment risk with their pension fund.

If you are **contracted in** to Serps, then each year your National Insurance contributions buy you a unit of Serps entitlement. At the moment, once the first Serps payment is made after retirement the amount increases in line with inflation each year.

But the government's handling of Serps has attracted a growing amount of criticism from pensions experts. A string of government decisions over the past couple of years have served to undermine the value of Serps and make it far less attractive. The move that has brought the most criticism is the decision by the Social Security minister, Peter Lilley, to change the way Serps entitlements are calculated, a move that will hit lower earners most. His changes mean that Serps benefits for people retiring after 2000 will be reduced significantly. By 2010 benefits will fall by £600m a year. This lowering of benefits will continue to hit people retiring over the ensuing 30 years. By 2020 the reduction will amount to £1.3bn a year, by 2030 it will be £2.5bn and by 2040 it will be £2.9bn. These figures are calculated at today's values.

The changes to the Serps benefit calculations are retrospective, which means people have made contributions based on benefit calculations that have now been thrown out and replaced by less generous ones.

Under the present method of calculating Serps entitlement a man earning £8,000 a year with 20 years to retirement would have his salary revalued to retirement using the growth in national average earnings, say 7 per cent, to give a figure of £30,957. From this would be deducted the lower earnings limit (£3,016) which is the amount below which no National Insurance contributions are paid. The lower earnings limit is also revalued to retirement before making the deduction, but at a projected rate of inflation, which is always 2 per cent below the earnings figure. In this case it would be 5 per cent, which gives £8,002. This is deducted from the earnings figure to give a basis for Serps benefit of £22,955. But after 6 April 2000 the lower earnings limit in each financial year will be deducted from the relevant earnings *before* revaluation to retirement age. Using the above figures this would mean subtracting £3,016 from £8,000 to give £4,984, which, revalued using national average earnings, would give £19,286 as the basis for Serps benefit. The changes will hit low earners, many of whom are women.

SWAPS

One of a number of financial tools invented during the 1980s, engineered to meet the increasingly complex needs of big business. But the sight of whizz kids making big profits for themselves and clients by using such schemes tempted some less than suitable users into the hothouse atmosphere of the City of London. Famous cases involved such organisations as

Hammersmith and Fulham Council, which were eventually banned from using swaps by the courts.

Companies who want to borrow money use **interest rate swaps** either to reduce the cost of borrowing or to match their interest payments to their expected income.

Swaps are based on the idea of **comparative advantage**. One company will be able to borrow money by issuing bonds on different rates and terms compared to another. For instance company A may want to borrow money on a fixed rate, which means it will be sure of how much its repayments on the bonds will be and can match these repayments with its income. But it may be able to issue bonds more cheaply if it pays a variable rate of interest. On the other hand company B may want variable rate finance but can only borrow on a fixed rate. Both would be better off by issuing the bonds they are able to, and then **swapping** their interest payments. Swaps are organised by merchant banks, which match one company with another.

T is for:

TAKEOVERS AND MERGERS

When one company wants to swallow up another it mounts a takeover or merger. Takeovers can either be **agreed** or **hostile**. Agreed takeovers are often invited and involve the board of the target company recommending the takeover offer to shareholders. A hostile bid is uninvited. The aggressor makes an offer to the target company's shareholders which it hopes they will accept.

Hostile bids often involve a bitter battle as both sides struggle to win the support of shareholders. The takeovers we hear most about are for public companies. The arguments tend to unfold in the business pages of the national press and often boil down to the strength of the personalities of the main dramatis personae. Perhaps the best recent example of this was the £3.3bn bid for hotel and catering group Forte by leisure group Granada. The bid was largely fought out on the strengths of the opposing bosses – the suave Rocco Forte on one side and the laid-back Gerry Robinson of Granada on the other. Such bids require each side to gang together with their teams of specialist banking, stockbroking and public relations advisers. There are numerous different interest groups which need to be persuaded that the opposing party in a hostile bid should accept defeat, be they the aggressor or defender. Ultimately, however, it is up to the shareholders to decide who wins by accepting or rejecting an offer. Shareholders are either private individuals or the fund managers of the big institutions and pension funds, known as 'the institutions'. It is often this latter group who can decide if a bid is successful or not. They own large blocks of shares and their support for or opposition to a bid can prove conclusive.

Mergers are almost always agreed amicably between both sides.

A company may want to take over another for various reasons. The main reasons are:

- To increase market share.
- To diversify into a new line of business.
- To improve an ailing, badly managed business and realise its hidden value.
- To sell off a company bit by bit for more than its purchase price, known as **asset stripping**.
- A company which finds itself the target of a hostile takeover can itself bid for a third company as a defence to stave off unwelcome approaches. Another defence tactic is to go for the **scorched earth** approach. This involves selling off or at least threatening to sell off your best assets before a hostile bid is successful.
- Sometimes a company is invited to act as a **white knight**. A target company in a hostile bid will ask a third company, offering a more palatable alternative to the hostile bidder, to bid for it.

Takeovers and mergers are not subject to any statutory control but are overseen by the **Panel on Takeovers and Mergers (POTAM)** – a group of City grandees nominated by the Bank of England and other financial institutions. It publishes the **Takeover Code** and gives quick rulings on contentious matters during a bid. But if there are no statutory rules how does it enforce its decisions and the terms of the Takeover Code? The answer is, through sanctions. If an organisation flouts the Code then it will find itself snubbed by the rest of the City. This may not sound much but it is very serious. City firms will refuse to deal with the organisation, leaving it unable to carry on its day-to-day business or continue with a bid. The financial regulators can force their member firms not to co-operate with a company in breach of the Code. The message is: observe the Code or see your business paralysed.

People should not confuse the POTAM with the **Monopolies and Mergers Commission (MMC)**. The POTAM regulates the conduct of a bid, whereas the MMC is a government organisation that assesses the public interest and anti-competitive effects of a takeover or merger. The process starts with the Office of Fair Trading, which may refer a bid to the Secretary of State for Trade and Industry if there are consumer interest implications. The Secretary of State may then pass it to the MMC if:

- the combined organisation controls at least 25 per cent of a market (deemed to be a monopoly);
- the takeover is of assets worth more than £70m; or
- the bid is against the public interest.

The MMC will duly report on a bid. If cleared the bid can go through. If not the MMC will recommend that the bid should be blocked. It is then at the minister's discretion whether the bid continues or not.

TAXATION

The American politician **Benjamin Franklin** said that in life there is nothing certain but death and taxes. In Britain most of our tax is collected by the Inland Revenue – nearly £80bn a year of it.

The 1996–97 tax year sees the introduction of a new regime called **self-assessment**, which will allow nine million people to calculate their own tax bills. This might seem like an invitation to fiddle the Revenue, but in fact self-assessment will create a tougher regime for would-be tax evaders. The system will affect anyone who receives a tax return. This means that higher-rate taxpayers, company directors, the self-employed, freelancers, and anyone with investment income not taxed at source will be included.

Self-assessment involves a role reversal. Instead of completing a tax return and getting a bill in return from the Revenue, people will calculate their own return and send their assessment with a cheque to the Revenue. This all sounds very civilised but delays in completing returns and any attempts at deliberate evasion will be punished severely. Under the new regime taxpayers have nine months after the end of a tax year to submit their assessments – three months longer than previously. The deadline will therefore be 31 January each year. People can still choose to have their bills calculated by the Revenue but must submit their returns by five months after the end of the tax year, giving them one month less than previously. The final deadline for this option will be 30 September.

The Revenue says it will be lenient with mathematical slip-ups as it can make changes to minor mistakes within nine months of a return being filed. Taxpayers will be able to make changes during the 12 months after submitting a return.

Failure to submit an assessment on time will trigger a series of penalties, as follows:

1. An immediate £100 fine.
2. A further £100 fine after a six-month delay.
3. Daily fines of £60 for continued delay.
4. Delays of more than a year will result in fines levied in proportion to the amount of tax outstanding in addition to the fines.

Taxpayers are responsible for obtaining tax returns. Not receiving one is no excuse under the new regime.

There will also be a series of separate fines for late payments:

1. Immediate interest charges on amount overdue.
2. A 5 per cent surcharge on tax that is more than 28 days late.
3. A further 5 per cent surcharge on tax that is unpaid six months after the due date.
4. Additional interest charged on all outstanding amounts of tax and surcharges.

The Revenue has promised a new style tax return to make the move to self-assessment as simple as possible. It will be split into schedules covering all the different possibilities, such as one for the self-employed, one for pensions income, one for savings income and so on. People simply fill in the relevant schedules.

People will also be expected to provide details of any benefits they receive from their employers such as medical insurance. If this all sounds too complicated for words, then people can still ask their accountant to sort things out for them – for a fee, of course.

TESSA

Introduced in 1991 by the then Chancellor of the Exchequer, John Major, Tessa stands for **Tax Exempt Special Savings Account**. The accounts allow each adult to save a total of £9,000 in a tax-free deposit account offered by banks and building societies. The schemes have proved popular and about £25bn has been deposited. To benefit from the tax-exempt status, the money must not be withdrawn before the five-year period is over.

The first Tessas were taken out by people in January 1991 and matured in 1996. Many people have been asking themselves what they should do with the proceeds. In the 1994 Budget, the chancellor Kenneth Clarke, announced that new Tessas would be available from January 1996. This means that people can roll over their original £9,000 stake into a new tax-free account, but not the accumulated interest. Once an existing Tessa matures, then the interest earned is liable to tax.

Under the pre-1996 Tessa rules a person with a maturing account would be limited to a first-year deposit of £3,000, then £1,800 for each of the next three years, and £600 in the final year. However, the chancellor has decided to raise the first-year deposit limit for a second Tessa to allow individuals to invest the full £9,000 straight away as long as they open a second Tessa within six months of maturity. People who invest less than £9,000 initially can continue to invest in subsequent years up to the £1,800 annual limit. Others who have not previously had a Tessa, or who invested less than £3,000 in the first year of their original Tessa, will be limited to £3,000 in the first year of their new 1996 Tessa.

When Tessas were first launched in 1991, base rates were as high as 14 per cent. Most Tessas were taken out on a variable rate of interest, so the amount of interest earned has fallen over the years. The best performers have been those Tessas launched with a fixed rate of interest which have been protected against falling rates. If interest rates rise over the next five years a variable-rate Tessa would work out best. If rates stay more or less the same, a fixed-rate Tessa may prove more attractive depending on the rate on offer.

The past five years have shown that savers who chose a Tessa from one of the big high-street banks have lost out on nearly £1,000 each compared with the best performing variable-rate Tessas. The best variable rates over the whole five-year period have come from the smaller building societies and banks. They have kept rate cuts to a minimum to remain competitive, whereas the big banks have been less worried about passing on the full effects of base-rate cuts.

TIMESHARE

People who sell timeshare have in the past been considered

much lower down the evolutionary tree than both the vendor of second-hand cars and the person telephoning to sell double glazing.

Timeshare schemes involve people buying a one- or two-week stay each year in a particular resort – a bit like owning your own holiday home but without the choice of when to go and stay. But the industry has had its problems, hence the reputation. Difficulties have centred on the way timeshare is sold with legions of commission-hungry salespeople browbeating potential customers into buying properties they neither want nor need – then refusing to refund their money when they complain.

The problems were such that in 1990 the Office of Fair Trading launched an inquiry into the timeshare business, and in 1993 Parliament passed the Timeshare Act. This introduced the idea of a cooling-off period whereby people had 14 days to change their mind about a purchase without losing out. The Timeshare Council has also been set up to protect both consumer and business interests; it has a series of disciplinary measures it can mete out to members who fail to comply, including expulsion.

The big advantage of timeshare these days is the flexibility that has been introduced into the scheme. No longer are people locked into the same property or holiday period year in, year out. There are exchange organisations that allow people to swap their timeshare allocations. These exchanges work by timeshare owners 'banking' their week in the exchange firm's computers and requesting alternatives in other resorts. A fee is payable for arranging an exchange, as well as an annual membership fee for joining an exchange organisation.

As well as swapping timeshares, people can buy and sell them. There are now a number of resale businesses that act pretty much like estate agents. Sellers put their weeks on their books and buyers choose from the timeshares on offer. Prices through this resale market can be much cheaper than buying timeshares new from the developers.

An alternative to the timeshare idea is the **holiday bond**, which involves people buying into a property-based insurance bond, and receiving 'free' holidays each year in return. Money from investors is pooled to buy bricks and mortar. If property values rise, so too does the value of each investor's holding.

But the difference compared with more usual property investments is that the fund manager only buys holiday villas and apartments – and investors earn the right to use the properties whenever there is space available. These schemes allocate investors with a holiday point for every pound invested. Charts included in the brochures for these schemes show how many points are required for each week in any particular location. For example, this might be 600 points for a week in December in a one-bedroom villa to 15,200 points for a week in July or August in a four-bedroom, three-bathroom villa with a pool, both in Portugal. Someone who invests £5,000 is given 5,000 points in their first year and at least this number each year afterwards. So investors can afford the same standard of accommodation each year regardless of inflation. Points not used in one year are added to the next year's allocation.

The problem with these insurance bond-based schemes are the charges, which can be quite high, and the fact that you are unlikely to make any capital growth on your investment.

TRAVEL INSURANCE

This form of insurance is taken out by holidaymakers to protect themselves against mishaps such as cancellations, losing personal goods like cameras, mislaying traveller's cheques or having any of these items stolen. The cover also protects them against illness and the cost of hospital treatment while abroad. Regular travellers can cover themselves all year round through an **annual policy**, while people who make just one trip a year can buy a policy simply to cover a two-week package holiday.

Most people buy the travel insurance offered by their tour

Travel insurance protects you against mishaps such as cancellations or losing personal goods

operator or travel agent, but this can be a lot more expensive than buying it separately from a specialist travel insurance firm or broker. In fact, travel insurance policies are sold by banks, building societies and the Post Office.

Many people already have travel insurance but do not know it. Many gold cards offer travel insurance, as do some home contents policies, which will extend to possessions taken abroad in your baggage.

Medical bills and theft produce the most claims under travel insurance policies. These policies will also provide cash for each day spent in hospital as well as paying the medical bills. However, fraudulent claims on travel policies tend to centre on claims of theft. As a result insurers will only provide the value of what you have lost allowing for wear and tear. They are unlikely to pay more than £250–£350 per item. Money and traveller's cheques are insured separately, and tickets are often also included under this heading.

TRAVELLER'S CHEQUES

Plastic cards are rapidly taking over as the holidaymaker's preferred means of spending whilst abroad. But many still take traveller's cheques, either as a back-up payment method, or in combination with plastic and Eurocheques.

Traveller's cheques can be bought in sterling or foreign currencies. Their biggest advantage is that they can be quickly replaced if they are lost or stolen. You should also be able to get a better exchange rate than you would for currency.

If travelling to the United States, it is better to take dollar cheques, as few places will exchange sterling. The cheques can often be used as if they were ordinary money, with change given in cash. In Europe, the choice of denomination depends partly on how you think exchange rates will move during the holiday.

Some foreign exchange bureaux charge commission. But those that do not may offer inferior exchange rates. Working out which to choose is therefore difficult for the less mathematically inclined. When exchanging for cash abroad, local banks tend to offer better deals than hotels or bureaux de change, but always compare rates first.

TRUSTS

One of the most efficient ways of avoiding, or reducing, **inheritance tax** is to shelter the relevant assets in a trust. It is also a useful way of avoiding income tax and capital gains tax.

Trustees are appointed to look after the assets held in a trust on behalf of the people who are supposed to benefit from the trust's proceeds, known as the **beneficiaries**. Trustees are the **legal** owners of the trust's assets and are obliged to act in the best interests of the beneficiaries.

Never set up a trust without professional advice. Trustees should be given the widest possible powers of investment and delegation and the terms should be as flexible as possible in case of unforeseen eventualities. Once created, a trust is almost always irrevocable, even if the person who set up the trust (the **donor**) is also a trustee, although it may be possible to secure a variation on the original terms through the courts.

There are several types of trust. The main ones are:

- **Accumulation and maintenance trust** These minimise inheritance tax, normally for the benefit of children and grandchildren. The income may be used for education and maintenance among other things, and advances may be granted on request.
- **Absolute trust** A useful tool in the avoidance of income tax and capital gains tax (CGT). It gives beneficiaries sole entitlement to both income and capital, with the proceeds payable at age 18. For inheritance tax purposes, the assets are a **potentially exempt transfer**, which means they are tax-free after seven years.
- **Interest in possession trust** This trust pays income to named beneficiaries. The capital may be paid to a second named beneficiary on the death of the first – a child on the death of the mother, for instance. Useful for inheritance tax planning or CGT avoidance.
- **Discretionary trust** It allows trustees to pay income or capital to people in a specified category such as children, or grandchildren. May be used to save income tax, CGT and inheritance tax.

$\mathcal{U}$ is for:

UNIT TRUSTS

A simple way for people to play the stock market, regardless of whether they have big or small sums to invest. There are now 6.6 million people who own unit trusts, with investments worth £113bn. A unit trust pools lots of savers' money together into one big fund. A professional fund manager invests this pool on behalf of investors who are known as **unit holders**. People can buy and sell their units at any time. The price of units is determined by dividing the value of the fund by the number of units in issue. The unit price is calculated on a daily basis and published in the business pages of the national press.

The main advantages of unit trusts are convenience and risk reduction. The trusts work by following the proverbial advice of not putting all your eggs in one basket. Instead of investing in a handful of shares – a strategy which could prove costly if one of the shares does badly – unit holders buy a stake in dozens, sometimes hundreds, of companies through the unit trust. This reduces the impact on the portfolio of one or two poor performing shares. It would be impossible for individuals to buy a similar size portfolio of shares for themselves unless they had sums of at least £50,000 to invest on the stock market.

There are more than 1,400 unit trusts which allow you to spread your risk across a variety of specific sectors

This is not to say investing smaller amounts directly in shares is a mistake. Most people, however, have neither the time nor inclination to go through the selection process, even with the help of a stockbroker.

There are more than 1,400 unit trusts to choose from, run by investment management companies big and small. The unit trust universe can be subdivided in a variety of ways and trusts cover every investment angle. Some offer portfolios that are designed to produce capital growth, others are run to produce income, with a third type designed to achieve both. To satisfy these aims some trusts are invested in shares, some in bonds or even cash, while some split their assets between all three. There are specialist unit trusts that invest in specific sectors such as property, telecommunications, health or mining, while others cover specific overseas stock markets as well as those covering the UK stock market. Other subdivisions include small companies trusts, unit trusts investing in warrants, and unit trusts that invest in derivatives such as futures and options.

Trust managers charge an initial fee of between 5 and 7 per cent plus an annual charge of 1 per cent or more. There is also a **bid offer spread**. This is the difference between the price at which you buy units and the price at which you could immediately sell them again. The buy price will be higher than the sell price. The bid offer spread quoted in the press includes the initial charge.

Two of the most successful types of unit trust over the past couple of years have been **index trackers** and **funds of funds**. As the name suggests index trackers follow the fortunes of a **stock market index** such as the FTSE 100 Index of leading UK shares. Or unit trusts can track the much broader UK index of the FT-A All Share, which covers all the quoted shares on the main London Stock Exchange. Funds of funds, on the other hand, are unit trusts that buy units in other unit trusts, providing the most diversified route into the world's stock markets.

Index trackers have found a new group of fans of late because investors have been getting increasingly disappointed with the performance of active fund managers – the people paid to pick shares that are supposed to produce superior returns compared to a relevant index. It is quite simple to build a portfolio of shares that will mirror the performance of an index. In its simplest form all you have to do is buy shares in each of the companies that make up any particular index. If a highly paid fund manager cannot even beat this simplistic approach to fund management, then why bother forking out the annual management fees? This disquiet over performance, and some aggressive marketing and highly competitive pricing by companies offering index tracker funds, has led to an upturn in the latter's fortunes. The main attraction of index trackers is their low-risk and low-cost approach to fund management, and the sad but true fact that many active fund managers cannot beat them.

Index tracking funds have less need for full-time fund managers or research departments because their portfolios are bought and sold according to a set plan. Once the shares have been bought they are only sold when the constituent parts of the index change. Their simplicity means they are ideal for the first-time investor unsure about how to pick a good trust out of the thousands available. The low charges on index trackers are also good news for the uninitiated unit trust investor, as more money is invested from day one and less is taken out along the way. It is high annual management charges that can take the heaviest toll on performance over the long term, not the initial charges.

Not all index trackers will follow a given index with the same degree of accuracy. Funds tracking the FTSE 100 will have differing performance if they have different charges. The higher the charges, the less accurate the tracking. Also, the method of tracking can have an impact on performance. As well as buying every share that makes up an index, a tracker fund could buy a representative sample of the index calculated mathematically to replicate the index's performance. Another alternative is to use **derivatives** such as index futures.

Funds of funds unit trusts are also good for first-time investors, and they also have a useful tax advantage for investors looking for a simple way to run a large, regularly traded portfolio. Investors buy units in a trust which then buys units in other unit trusts. The idea is to provide as wide a diversification as possible by investing in a wide range of funds run by a wide range of fund managers. A fund of funds unit trust can offer investors exposure to the fortunes of thousands of shares in any number of different stock markets around the world. They do not have to be invested solely in shares either. They can add bonds and cash to their portfolios.

There are two basic types of fund of funds. The first is run by a fund management group which uses it to buy units in its other, in-house unit trusts. The obvious drawback with a fund like this is that investors are limiting themselves to just one company's funds, and very few unit trust companies have strong fund management performance in all markets. The second type is run by a fund manager to invest in the units of any unit trust. Clearly this latter type offers the chance of superior returns.

One snag that is common to both types is relatively high charges. As large buyers of another fund manager's units, they are in a position to negotiate down the initial charge when it comes to making an investment. But they are unlikely to be able to do anything about the annual management charge. So investors end up paying the charges on the fund of fund itself as well as the charges on the underlying funds, which can be a problem.

That said, as a portfolio management tool they are very useful. When a unit trust sells a holding, it is exempt from capital gains tax. Such a charge only arises with a unit trust when unit holders come to sell their units. Any dealing within the fund escapes the taxman's clutches. This means it is possible to transfer a portfolio of shares or other unit trusts into a well-diversified fund of funds and make switches without having to pay capital gains tax, unlike a normal portfolio.

More details are available from the Association of Unit Trusts and Investment Funds.

UNSECURED LOANS

These are a common means of buying consumer goods such as cars, holidays or household items. As the name suggests, borrowers do not have to offer assets as security against non-payment, as they would with a **secured loan**.

Unsecured loan rates tend to be higher than those for secured loans because of the greater perceived risk to lenders. The cost of a loan depends on the amount borrowed, the repayment period, and, often, on what the money is to be spent. Rates vary, so prospective borrowers should shop around. Look out for special offers, especially around August to catch new-reg car buyers and holidaymakers and January for the sales. Take note also of the **annual percentage rate (APR)**, which takes into account all the charges attached to the loan, rather than just the flat rate.

Unsecured loans normally involve a shorter repayment period than secured loans. They are usually available up to £15,000 and repayment is over a fixed period of between one and five years.

The interest rate is likely to be fixed at the start. This is good for borrowers who wish to know exactly how much money they will have to find each month, but bad if the prevailing interest rate plunges during the repayment period, as it did a few years ago.

Watch out especially for deductions for **payment protection insurance**. This finances loan repayments if unemployment strikes. But premiums are pretty hefty and there are often so many exclusions in the small print that the policy would not pay out in many cases. You may find premium payments are automatically added to your monthly repayment bill unless you specifically state otherwise.

$\mathcal{V}$ is for:

VALUE ADDED TAX

This tax is collected by suppliers of goods and services on behalf of Customs and Excise. The current rate on all but a few **exempt,** or **zero-rated,** goods is 17.5 per cent. Insurance, finance and education are all exempt; food, children's clothing, books and newspapers are zero-rated. The only other exception is domestic fuel and power, whose rate was pegged at 8 per cent following a wave of protest among pensioners and similar groups.

VAT is collected at every stage in the goods and services distribution chain. Businesses must register for VAT if their **annual taxable turnover** is above the VAT threshold, currently £46,000. It may be worth registering even when turnover is lower than the threshold in order to reclaim the VAT on various goods and services. Registration is also probably necessary for people who purchase goods from other EC countries, whatever their earnings.

Customs and Excise pick up the excess between the VAT paid out and the VAT collected. There are various ways of paying it. You can, for instance, fill in a VAT return every quarter and pay the surplus to the department, or you can opt to complete an annual return, provided your taxable turnover is less than £300,000. If you pay more VAT than you collect, you will get a refund.

VAT is a self-employed person's nightmare. Valuable time has to be spent updating records and making sure that they are as clear and accurate as possible. A record must be kept of all the tax paid and received, plus a summary of VAT for each tax period covered by the tax returns. This summary is called the VAT account. Business accounts must by law be kept for five years from the date on which the annual tax return is due back. VAT registered businesses normally have to keep records for six years.

Customs and Excise gives the following tips to new registrants:

- Record all business transactions.
- Keep documents like receipts, bills, bank statements, and cheque stubs.
- Keep business and personal finance separate.

VENTURE CAPITAL TRUSTS

Invented by the chancellor, Kenneth Clarke, in his 1994 Budget as a way of increasing investment in small, private companies, venture capital trusts offer people a convenient and easily tradable investment route into **unquoted** companies. Such investments offer the potential for superior returns, although venture capital is a risky business. However, the trusts' portfolio approach reduces this risk by spreading investments among a large number of private companies.

To encourage investors to back the trusts the government offers tax breaks on investments of up to £100,000. It gives up-front income tax relief of 20 per cent plus the chance to defer capital gains tax on existing investments which are sold and transferred into the shares of a trust. The CGT tax bill on these transferred investments becomes payable when shares in the venture capital trust (VCT) are sold. There is no CGT payable on any profits made on the shares themselves and

VCT investments are also free of income tax.

VCT shares are quoted on the London Stock Exchange and can be bought or sold at any time. The trusts are allowed to invest a maximum of £1m per tax year in any one company. A private company's gross assets must be no more than £10m before a VCT invests in it and no more than £11m after. No single holding in a company can exceed 15 per cent of a trust's value and a trust must distribute 85 per cent of its income to investors. The trusts have also been made exempt from corporation tax. After three years, at least 70 per cent by value of a VCT's investments must be in qualifying, unquoted holdings. The remainder must be in quoted ordinary shares or fixed interest securities.

The trusts are more attractive than their predecessor, the business expansion scheme (BES), which had only limited success in providing investment funds for growing businesses. The listing of venture capital trusts on the Stock Exchange means people will be able to sell their holdings at any time – a big advantage over BES. The VCT shares are said to be **liquid** or easily tradable as a result. Investors know there will always be a buyer for their VCT shares, although the price offered may be less than the price investors bought at. Many BES were launched by accountancy firms and law firms, which were good at taking advantage of tax breaks but not so successful at spotting good investments. The venture capital trusts that have been launched and those that are planned for 1996 have been put together by investment groups with more experience of unquoted companies.

Venture capital trusts are not the only way people can invest money in unquoted or very small companies. A very large and important sector of the **investment trust industry** is devoted to venture capital deals, while a more direct approach can be had through the **enterprise investment scheme (EIS)**. Also, companies that arrange for a listing on the **Alternative Investment Market (AIM)** are generally small or relatively new companies seeking to expand fast.

W *is for:*

WARRANTS

These give people the chance to add spice to their portfolios at very little cost, but tend to bring the worst out in the private investor. This is because warrants have fallen into the hands of people who do not really understand what they have got.

Warrants allow investors to buy a certain number of a company's shares at a fixed price at a fixed time in the future. They are issued both by investment trusts and trading companies such as BTR and Eurotunnel. Warrants are either handed out free to investors as part of a new share issue or can be bought on the stock market, as they are quoted securities in their own right.

People like to own warrants for one of the following reasons:

- To sell in the market and receive the going price if the warrant price rises.
- To combine warrants with a low-risk portfolio of gilts or other bonds to provide extra growth potential.
- To keep the warrant with the intention of **exercising** it.

An investor exercises a warrant when he or she wants to take up his or her right to buy the underlying shares. An investor who does this must have the capital to pay for the shares. The price they pay for these shares is fixed by the terms and conditions of the warrant and is called the **exercise price** or **strike price**. Exercising a warrant normally only becomes worthwhile if the cost of the warrant plus its exercise price is *less* than the price of the ordinary shares in the market. So if a company's warrants have an exercise price of 200p and the ordinary shares in the market are trading at 225p, then it is worthwhile exercising the warrants and subscribing for more shares, as an immediate profit of 25p per share is available. In this case the warrants are said to have an **intrinsic value** of 25p.

In a small number of circumstances it is worth exercising a warrant when the exercise price is *above* the ordinary share price. This happens when the exercise price and the ordinary share price are close together and the cost of buying the shares through a stockbroker, including dealing commission, is higher than exercising the warrants.

The most common issuers of warrants are investment trusts. While warrants give holders the *right* to buy a trust's shares they do not impose an *obligation* on the investor to do so. Warrants do not always have to be exercised on a specific date in the future. Sometimes they can be exercised during a specific period, such as three weeks.

The big attraction of warrants is that they give investors exposure to the performance of a trust's shares but at a fraction of the cost of the shares. Warrant holders do not receive dividends. Many recent investment trust issues have handed out free warrants – normally one free warrant for every five ordinary shares – as a sweetener to try and make sure the trust launch goes with a bang.

Exercising a warrant means new shares have to be issued to satisfy the warrant-related demand. This can dilute the trust's **net asset value (NAV)**. Investors may well see investment trusts publish two sets of performance figures, showing both its net asset value assuming all outstanding warrants were exercised – the **diluted NAV** – and the **undiluted NAV**, which makes no allowance for the effect of warrants.

Two other important terms to remember are warrant **gearing** and warrant **premium**. Gearing is expressed as a ratio – the share price divided by the warrant price. If the share price is 150p and the warrant 45p, the gearing is 3.3. This figure tells investors that the warrant gives them full exposure to the fortunes of the shares but at only one-third of their cost. The higher the gearing the more exposure at a fraction of the cost. This means more cash is available to invest in safer investments.

A warrant's premium is the percentage by which the warrant price plus the exercise price exceeds the share price. If the exercise price is 100p and the warrant price is 44p with a share price of 120p the premium is 20 per cent (24 as a percentage of 120). In this case the shares would have to rise by 20 per cent before it becomes worthwhile to exercise the warrants. Warrants that are worth exercising are said to be **in-the-money**, and those that are not are said to be **out-of-the-money**.

Sadly, warrants have proved a little too complicated for some investors to understand. The popular Mercury World Mining investment trust gave investors one warrant with every five ordinary shares. The warrants became exercisable in April 1995 and had an exercise price of 100p. In other words, people could buy the trust's shares for 100p by exercising the warrants. This would have made sense had the shares been trading at more than 100p. In fact, when the exercise date came, the shares were trading at 85p.

To exercise the warrants and pay 100p for shares that could be bought in the stock market for 85p is investment madness. But many private investors, confused by their warrants, did exactly that, spending £250,000 on shares that made them an immediate loss of 14.5p a share. They also lost their right to sell the warrants themselves in the market. At the time, the price of the warrants was 20p each, which means that the confused warrant investors lost out twice to the tune of 34.5p a share.

WILLS

Once children are involved things become a little more complicated

Make a Will Week is now an established annual event when the legal profession try and persuade people of the importance of making a will. But despite this, more than half of the adults in Britain still do not bother to make a will.

There is no point making a will if you have no assets but once you do own something such as a house it is always worthwhile making a will, if only to make sure your possessions go to those people you really want them to go to. Wills are also part of inheritance tax planning, and in addition, allow you to specify who should handle your affairs after your death.

People who die without a will are said to die **intestate**. This is not such a problem for a married couple without children, as possessions will normally pass to the spouse in this case and no inheritance tax is payable on transfers between spouses. Once children are involved things become a little more complicated. If a father dies intestate his estate will be divided up between his wife and children according to the rules of intestacy, which is not much use to the person who intended to leave everything to his wife. Also, common law partners may lose all the assets intended for them to the relatives of the deceased if he fails to make a will.

A simple will costs between £75 and £100. There are a number of ways a will can be drawn up. The most common method is to use a solicitor, although there is no guarantee of finding a good one. There are specialist will-writing companies, although again their quality varies. People can also try drawing up their own wills. Do-it-yourself will-writing packs are available from the Post Office and large stationers. Other useful information is available from the Consumer's Association.

WITH-PROFITS

A traditional method of investing, which has been used by insurance companies for decades and is normally linked to regular premium endowment policies or single premium investment bonds, the with-profits approach requires people to tie up money for at least five years, usually more. In return, they buy into a stock market investment that removes much of the usual risk and volatility of share-based portfolios.

People who buy a with-profits investment are signing a contract agreeing to invest a certain amount of money over a specific period. If they break the contract by demanding their money back before the end of the term they will receive a **surrender value**. In the early years of a with-profits investment these surrender values may be less than people contributed. As years go on, surrender values will remain less than their investment would be worth if they were left alone.

With-profits investments are pooled into a with-profits fund. This is then invested in a broad range of shares, gilts and property. These returns are passed on to with-profits investors once a year in the form of an **annual bonus**. These bonuses are reviewed each year. Once they have been granted they are guaranteed by the insurance company operating the with-profits scheme.

The direct comparison is with the other main form of collective investment – **unit linked**. With a unit-linked policy or bond (or unit trust, which works using exactly the same principle), returns are added up daily, with performance being reflected in a daily price. Unit-linked investments are exposed to the full effects of stock-market ups and downs and can therefore prove highly volatile. In contrast, a with-profits investment smooths out these ups and downs. When an annual bonus is paid, not all returns are given to policyholders. Some are kept in reserve. This means that in bad years when stock markets fall or fail to rise there is always something in the bonus kitty to pay to investors. Conversely, in good years more can be kept in reserve to build up a layer of fat that investors can draw on when things are lean. Bonuses may rise and fall from year to year but at least investors know there will be some growth each year, something that is far from certain with unit-linked and other stock-market investments.

This approach means in a year when the stock market soars, with-profits investors will do well but may underperform unit-linked investors. But, of course, in a year when the market falls or is disappointing, with-profits investors who can draw on reserves are likely to do better. Over the long term this approach has led to with-profits investors often beating unit-linked counterparts.

As well as annual bonuses, with-profits contracts may also pay a **terminal bonus** when the investments mature further, boosting returns. The longer the investment is held for, the higher the terminal bonus.

In the past, most with-profits business was arranged on a

regular premium basis. Over the last few years many of the leading insurers have started to offer with-profits as a single premium bond, which has attracted a lot of building society investors looking for above inflation returns. Certainly with-profits has produced impressive results. The *average* returns on a 25-year with-profits endowment have been steady at about 12.7 per cent after basic rate tax.

X *is for:*

EX AND CUM PRICES

These terms refer to shares or bonds and relate to the rights associated with those securities – normally dividend payments or extra share issues. If a share price published in the newspaper has xd next to it, this stands for ex-dividend. Investors who buy shares xd will not be entitled to the next dividend payment. This is a stock-market settlement detail. Once a company announces it is to pay a dividend and the date of that payment, the Stock Exchange selects a cut-off point after which new shareholders will not earn the dividend. The cut-off point is known as the **xd date**. Once the dividend is paid the xd period finishes. In the same way, when a company announces it is to issue new shares through a rights issue there is a cut-off date after which new shareholders will not qualify. This is the ex-rights date shown as xr next to a share price.

The opposite of xd and xr are cum dealings. Cum means including any rights. As most shares on the stock market are cum dividend or cum rights the term is not usually printed next to a share price. It is assumed a share or bond is dealing cum rights unless otherwise stated.

$\mathcal{Y}$ is for:

YIELD

This is the technical term for the income people earn from their investments. Yields are applied to shares, bonds – both fixed interest and variable rate – and bank and building society deposits.

Yield is always expressed as a percentage. To calculate a yield, take the amount of gross income earned and divide it by the market price of the share or bond and multiply by 100. Market price and yield have an inverse relationship. As the price of a bond or share rises, the yield from the interest or dividend falls and vice versa. A yield from a deposit account is simply the amount of interest paid.

The City also talks about the **yield curve**. The big commercial banks pay different rates of interest depending on the length of large deposits made with them by other financial institutions. They pay low rates on deposits held in overnight accounts and steadily higher ones on deposits held for one month, three months, six months and so on. This reflects the money market's belief that interest rates are likely to rise over time. This series of rising rates is the yield curve. If money markets believe interest rates are going to fall in the long term, the yield curve will turn **negative**, with rates for long-term deposits lower than shorter-term deposits.

Z is for:

ZEROS

The shorthand description for zero-coupon bonds or zero-dividend preference shares (zdps). Zero-coupon bonds are bonds that do not pay interest in the normal way. There is no coupon or fixed interest payment every six months as with conventional bonds.

In the same way, zdps – issued by investment trusts – are shares that do not pay half-yearly dividends like ordinary shares. Instead zeros have a fixed life and a maturity value. They are issued at the start of their life at a deep discount to their final maturity value. All investors have to do is buy the zeros at the outset and hold them to maturity, when they will receive a predetermined payout. This gives them a known profit over the term of the zero, which can be expressed as an annual percentage rate of growth.

Although issuers of zeros tell investors what return they can expect when their investments mature, there are no guarantees. Investors in zdps (or their advisers) need to keep an eye on how well the current assets of the issuing investment trust or company cover the final repayment. They also need to be aware of by how much the assets can fall before the final repayment is in jeopardy. For instance, the assets of an investment trust with three years to maturity may be able to shrink by 5 per cent a year before the final payout on the zdps is in jeopardy, thanks to previous years of strong growth.

That said, even if an investment trust does not have sufficient assets to repay the full amount of a zdp on maturity it may well repay something, although not what investors may have been expecting.

As far as tax is concerned, the position is somewhat unclear at the moment for holders of zero-coupon bonds. Tax experts are awaiting clarification from the Inland Revenue, although they expect private investors will be asked to pay income tax at their marginal rate based on their actual return. Private investors with zdps pay capital gains tax on sale or redemption of the shares. There is a technical liability to income tax, but as there is no income paid, there is no tax payable.

The Budget 1995

Budgets always create a great deal of hyperbole ahead of the actual House of Commons speech delivered by the Chancellor of the Exchequer. The media whips itself into a lather of speculation, much of which proves wrong. It also devotes thousands of column inches and hours of air time to advice for the benefit of the incumbent chancellor.

As well as the media there is a well-tuned lobbying business that presents the special pleading of every conceivable interest group in the country from wine makers to plastic bag makers to money makers. All this despite the fact that the chancellor has very little room to manoeuvre, being constrained by the country's big political and economic concerns.

But why do we have Budgets and how significant are they? The Budget presented by the Chancellor of the Exchequer is similar to any household budget. It is a statement to the nation showing how much the government spends, how much it earns and how much it needs to borrow. If any of these figures are out of kilter the Budget will also contain proposals on how to change any or all of these things.

These proposals are officially put forward in the Finance Bill each year, which is debated by MPs. If it passes through Parliament it then becomes a Finance Act and the proposals become a reality. Until recently the Budget was held in March and did not contain any of the government's spending plans, but rather how the government proposed to raise more or less revenue. Instead, spending plans were contained in the **Autumn Statement**. However, the spending and revenue raising sides of the government finances have been united and the whole complex equation is presented in a unified Budget now held in November.

As the Budget is the event when tax and spending plans are changed it can take on a lot of political significance, particularly in the year before a general election. It is with these Budgets that governments can be at their most generous in terms of decreasing tax or increasing spending to help boost their standing in the opinion polls. At Budgets just after elections they can afford unpopular measures, safe in the knowledge that they can always turn the tide with a few useful tax wheezes in Budgets to come.

The government uses the Budgets to change not only its own finances but also those of industry as well as private individuals. It is the time when the economic tool box is opened up to the chancellor. He can turn whatever economic handles or wheels are needed to achieve his Party's political objectives, which is why the Budget is so significant.

As far as the economy as a whole is concerned, the chancellor will reveal how much the government needs to borrow over the next two to three years to fund the **public sector borrowing requirement (PSBR)** – the amount added to the total **National Debt** every year. He will reveal plans for bringing the PSBR back into the black. To do so he will either have to announce tax increases or cuts in state spending overall. He can also use the Budget to reveal the government's thinking on general economic policy, and he will comment on the rate of inflation and give clues as to the likely next move in interest rates.

The nearer you get to an election the priority to cut tax has always been a driving force behind the chancellor's thinking. Conversely, when there are still a few years to go to the next election the public finances can be brought back under control by cuts in spending or tax increases. What a chancellor can afford to do in a Budget can often dictate when the next general election will be.

For instance, in the 1995 Budget the chancellor, Kenneth

Clarke, was unable to cut taxes significantly because the government's debts were worse than expected. What tax cuts there were were modest, and politicians knew that they were not sufficient to restore the fortunes of the Conservative government after a series of previous Budgets that had raised taxes. Instead the chancellor put in place the first half of a two-part strategy that he hopes will allow him to deliver big tax cuts in November 1996, the last Budget before the general election which must be held in 1997.

Taxes are generally the issue people are most interested in when it comes to the Budget. These can be **direct** such as income tax, or they can be **indirect** such as value added tax or duty on spirits. Changes in these taxes tend to hit the headlines the morning after the Budget, as do big changes in spending priorities.

Below are detailed the main changes in the 1995 Budget that affect family finances.

INCOME TAX

The Conservative government's long-term goal is to reduce the basic rate of tax to 20p in the pound. With this in mind it implemented the following revisions:

- Increased the personal allowance before people pay any tax to £3,765, up from £3,525.
- Cut the basic rate of income tax from 25 per cent to 24 per cent.
- Included more people in the 20 per cent lower-rate tax band by increasing it to include £3,900 of earnings, an increase of £700.
- Increased the threshold above which higher-rate (40 per cent) tax is paid from £24,300 to £25,500.
- Married couples will find it slightly more lucrative to have tied the knot. They will receive an extra income tax-free

allowance of £1,790, compared to £1,720 before.

- A similar sum is available for single parents and widows.
- All age allowances have also increased. For married people aged between 65 and 74 the allowance has risen from £4,630 to £4,910. For married couples over 75 it has risen from £4,800 to £5,090. For single people aged between 65 and 74 the allowance has gone up from £4,630 to £4,910, while single people over 75 will get an allowance of £5,090 up from £4,800.

These measures will mean that 26 million taxpayers will pay less tax, and will ensure that 25 per cent of all taxpayers pay only 20 per cent. They will also take 220,000 people out of the tax net altogether.

CAPITAL GAINS TAX

A tax that the Conservative government would like to see abolished altogether, but 1995 was not the year to go the whole hog. Instead, a small number of measures were introduced to reduce the impact of the tax, which is charged at people's marginal rate of income tax:

- The annual allowance before which tax is charged on gains has been increased from £6,000 to £6,300.
- The age at which entrepreneurs qualify for retirement relief when they want to sell holdings in their own companies has been lowered from 55 to 50. They will now get full relief on gains of £250,000 plus half relief on gains between £250,000 and £1m.

INHERITANCE TAX (IHT)

The Conservatives fear many in 'middle Britain' will refuse to vote Tory because their relatively modest estates are being hit by death duties. This is another tax the Conservatives would like to see abolished. With this in mind the chancellor has taken the following steps:

- Increased the size of estate that escapes IHT – which is charged at 40 per cent – from £154,000 to £200,000.
- Given 100 per cent relief from IHT to shareholders in all qualifying unquoted companies.

These IHT measures mean an extra 7,500 estates will escape the tax and that a married couple can now shelter assets worth £400,000 from the tax compared to £308,000 before.

THE ELDERLY

The government announced a number of measures to try and ease the burden on people who have to pay for residential care in old age:

- The amount of assets an individual can own above which the state refuses to help meet the cost of long-term care was increased from £8,000 to £16,000.
- The point at which the state will pay for all the costs of long-term care was raised from £3,000 to £10,000 of assets.
- Benefits from long-term care insurance policies will be paid out free of tax.
- A consultative process was also announced to examine other ways of encouraging people to pay for their own long-term care. These include United States-style partnership schemes, where the state will agree to match any benefits bought by people from long-term care insurance policies, and ways of using pension fund assets to help pay for care.

INSURANCE

Along with long-term care policies, other insurance policies taken out by people to protect themselves against financial hardship will be able to pay out benefits tax-free. These are:

- mortgage protection;
- permanent health insurance; and
- creditor insurance.

INVESTMENTS

The tax on savings and investment income has been reduced to 20 per cent for basic-rate taxpayers. The chancellor introduced this measure to bring investment income into line with tax on share dividends. The new lower rate of tax will apply to:

- savings accounts with UK banks and building societies;
- distributions from unit trusts;
- gilts and corporate bonds; and
- purchased life annuities.

Basic-rate taxpayers will not have to claim this lower rate of tax back from the Revenue. It will be deducted at source by the savings institution.

SHARE SCHEMES

To encourage share ownership through the workplace the chancellor announced a number of changes for share-based savings schemes:

- Income tax relief for company share options where the total value of shares granted does not exceed £20,000.

- A reduction in the minimum contract period for save-as-you-earn and profit-related schemes from five to three years.
- A reduction in the minimum amount that can be saved in these schemes to £5.

FUEL

Tax on leaded, unleaded and super-unleaded petrol as well as diesel rose 3.5p a litre. The tax on super-unleaded petrol will go up a further 3.9p a litre from 15 May 1996.

TOBACCO

Tax on 20 cigarettes went up 15p, and 6p on a pack of five small cigars. A 25 gram pack of pipe tobacco went up 8p.

Useful Addresses

Association of British Insurers, 51 Gresham St,
London EC2V 7HQ. *Tel*: 0171 600 3333.

Association of Friendly Societies, Royex House,
Aldermanbury Sq, London EC2V 7HR.
Tel: 0171 606 1881.

Association of Investment Trust Companies (AITC),
Durrant House, 8–13 Chiswell St, London EC1Y 4YY.
Tel: 0171 588 5347.

Association of Unit Trust and Investment Funds (Autif),
65 Kingsway, London WC2B 6TD. *Tel*: 0181 207 1361
(8 a.m.–11 p.m., 7 days a week).

Banking Ombudsman, 70 Grays Inn Road,
London WC1X 8NB. *Tel*: 0171 404 9944.

British Insurance and Investment Brokers Association (Biiba),
Biiba House, 14 Bevis Marks, London EC3A 7NT.
Tel: 0171 623 9043.

Building Societies Ombudsman, Millbank Tower, Millbank,
London SW1P 4XS. *Tel*: 0171 931 0044.

Building Society Commission, 15 Gt Marlborough St,
   London W1V 2LL. *Tel*: 0171 437 6628.

Building Society Investor Protection Board, The Secretary,
   15 Gt Marlborough St, London W1V 2LL.
   Tel: 0171 437 6628.

Capital Taxes Office, Official List of Exemptions,
   Ferrers House, PO Box 38, Castle Meadow Road,
   Nottingham NG2 1BB. *Tel*: 0115 974 2222.

Department of Environment (Council Tax Charter),
   Publications Despatch Centre, Blackhorse Road,
   London SE99 7TP. *Tel*: 0181 691 9191.

Ethical Investment Research Information Service (EIRIS).
   Tel: 0171 735 1351.

Inland Revenue Adjudicator, Adjudicator's Office,
   3rd Floor, Haymarket House, 28 Haymarket,
   London SW1Y 4SP. *Tel*: 0171 930 2292.

Insurance Ombudsman, 31 Southampton Row,
   London WC1B 5HT. *Tel*: 0171 928 7600.

Investment Ombudsman, 6 Federicks Place,
   London EC2R 8BT. *Tel*: 0171 796 3065.

Investors Compensation Scheme, Gavrelle House,
   2–14 Bunhill Row, London EC1Y 8RA.
   Tel: 0171 626 8820.

London International Financial Futures and Options
   Exchange (Liffe), Liffe Shop, Canonbridge,
   London EC4R 3XX. *Tel*: 0171 623 0444.

Money Management Register of Fee-based Independent
   Financial Advisers. *Tel*: 01179 769 444.

National Association of Citizens Advice Bureaux, 115–123 Pentonville Road, London N1 9LZ. *Tel*: 0171 833 2181.

National Savings, Sales Information Unit, Lytham St Annes, Lancs FY0 1YN. *Tel*: 01645 645 000 (8.30 a.m.–5 p.m. Mon–Fri).

Occupational Pensions Advisory Service (Opas). *Tel*: 0171 233 8080.

Pensions Ombudsman, 6th Floor, 11 Belgrave Rd, London SW1V 1RB. *Tel*: 0171 834 9144.

Personal Investment Authority (PIA) Consumer Helpline, 7th Floor, 1 Canada Sq, Canary Wharf, London E14 5AZ. *Tel*: 0171 538 8860.

PIA Ombudsman, Centre Point, 103 New Oxford St, London WC1A 1QH. *Tel*: 0171 240 3838

ProShare, Library Chambers, 13–14 Basinghall St, London EC2V 5BQ. *Tel*: 0171 600 0984.

Racehorse Owners Association, 42 Portman Sq, London W1H 9FF. *Tel*: 0171 486 6977.

Safe Home Income Plans, 374–378 Ewell Rd, Surbiton, Surrey KT6 7BB. *Tel*: 0181 390 8166.

Securities and Investments Board (SIB), Gavrelle House, 2–14 Bunhill Row, London EC1Y 8RA. *Tel*: 0171 638 1240.

Society of London Theatre, Bedford Chambers, The Piazza, Covent Garden, London WC2E 8HQ. *Tel*: 0171 836 0971.

World Gold Council, Kings House, 10 Haymarket, London SW17 4BP. *Tel*: 0171 930 5171.

Index

Index

Index

Index

Index